Disaster Risk Management

Disaster Risk Management

Case Studies in South Asian Countries

Edited by

Huong Ha
School of Business
Singapore University of Social Sciences
Singapore

R. Lalitha S. Fernando
Department of Public Administration
University of Sri Jayewardenepura
Nugegoda, Sri Lanka

Sanjeev Kumar Mahajan
Himachal Pradesh University
Shimla (India)

BEP BUSINESS EXPERT PRESS

First published in 2019 by
Business Expert Press, LLC
222 East 46th Street, New York, NY 10017
www.businessexpertpress.com

ISBN-13: 978-1-94944-306-6 (paperback)
ISBN-13: 978-1-94944-307-3 (e-book)

Business Expert Press Economics and Public Policy Collection

Collection ISSN: 2163-761X (print)
Collection ISSN: 2163-7628 (electronic)

Cover and interior design by S4Carlisle Publishing Services Private Ltd.,
Chennai, India

First edition: 2019

10 9 8 7 6 5 4 3 2 1

Printed in the United States of America.

Abstract

This book is an outcome of research studies carried out by eminent scholars and practitioners in South Asian countries in the field of disaster risk management. The book discusses how different South Asian countries manage disasters and address challenges associated with them. The case studies presented in this book reflect *reality versus myth*. In the quest to improve the ground-level situation, it is pertinent to understand the interdisciplinary nature of approaches used to tackle the aftermath of disasters. This book provides a framework for making administration effective and improving mitigation and rehabilitation measures with a view to ensuring a safer life for citizens.

The key features of this book include (i) the adoption of critical and multidisciplinary approaches in discussing disaster-related problems and emerging issues; and (ii) the provision of insights into the approaches to address the challenges and issues of disaster risk management. The different stakeholders, practitioners, policy makers, and researchers will acquire a fuller and richer understanding of the various issues related to disaster risk management.

Keywords

disaster risk management; e-waste; health; IT; nuclear disaster; psychological impact; South Asia

Contents

Foreword

The Challenges of Disaster Risk Management[1]

Arnold M. Howitt

Harvard University and Tsinghua University

The chapters in this volume bring into sharp relief the ongoing challenges of preparing South Asia for the multiple disasters—typhoons, earthquakes, tsunamis, landslides, floods, droughts, and more—that threaten lives, livelihoods, property, community life, culture, and the environment. That focus is vitally needed. We live in an era in which, on the one hand, significant progress has been made in concentrating the attention of local, national, and international actors preparing for and managing the risks of disaster. On the other hand, disasters have increased in frequency and intensified because of changing patterns of human activity, social structure, and the environment.

Confronting those challenges, the world community has focused on a new paradigm reflected in the Hyogo framework and revised and extended in the Sendai framework. As developed, the idea of disaster risk *management* includes more than the reduction of disaster risk. It implies a comprehensive framework of risk management at three different stages of the disaster cycle—preparing before a disaster occurs, responding during an event, and recovering following the disaster, with feedback to the next stage of preparedness. The overall objective is *resilience*—resilient

[1]The author gratefully acknowledges Douglas Ahlers, Joseph Pfeifer, and David Giles for thoughtful comments on earlier drafts. Notwithstanding their advice, all remaining errors of commission or omission are strictly the responsibility of the author.

individuals, communities, and a society capable of adapting to the perhaps radically changed conditions following a major disaster shock.

Disaster Vulnerabilities

One essential element of disaster management is the careful analysis of societal vulnerabilities, whether widely distributed among the population, falling on particular subgroups in society, or localized in specific places. Who are the vulnerable? Where and how are they vulnerable? Understanding the sources of vulnerability and the people most likely to be exposed to risk is an important step in either averting disaster or mitigating the impact of a crisis event.

As the authors in this volume point out, social inequality significantly increases risk and vulnerability. The poor are far more susceptible to disaster because of danger inherent in their surroundings, the character of the physical structures in which they live and work, the weak capacity or neglect of the institutions that serve them, and their own lack of knowledge of ways to protect themselves. Gender and age differences intensify these vulnerabilities to disasters. Women, the elderly, and children frequently claim fewer resources in their families than the men, have fewer links to informal community networks, have less physical mobility, possess less knowledge of risk reduction and coping possibilities, and face greater danger of harassment or molestation in disaster shelters. The elderly are less able to manage reconstruction of damaged homes and are more susceptible to fraud by contractors. Minority status often increases vulnerability further. Prejudice against minorities deepens the impacts of poverty, gender, and age—and outright discrimination in the distribution of relief services and access to food, water, shelter, health care, and education may spike during disaster response and in a prolonged recovery period.

Separate from but intertwined with the effects of social inequality are locational impacts. Urbanization, migration, population increases, and physical development practices result in large numbers of people settling in dangerous places. Rapid expansion of cities has increased settlement in flood plains or areas vulnerable to earthquakes and landslides and in construction of housing that lacks protections from rising waters or seismic events. Isolated communities may face similar dangers, with the added problem of being at great distance from and perhaps inaccessible to potential sources of disaster aid.

As climate change progresses, the authors of this volume show, locational vulnerability will increase. Rising sea levels, augmented by the intensification of meteorological events such as typhoons and intense rainstorms, will increase flood and wind dangers in cities and other settlements or create them in areas that have never faced them before. Climate change will also create slow-moving, chronic disasters, including threats to water supply and agricultural production. Saltwater intrusion will contaminate arable land; rising temperatures will cause more frequent drought, damaging the conditions for growing crops for human and animal food supply and other economic purposes. Rising temperatures will also cause human health problems: heat exhaustion, dehydration, respiratory and cardiovascular diseases, and increases in vector-borne illness.

Social Structure and Institutions

Vulnerability, as an author in this volume notes, is not only the result of risk at a particular location but also the result of the level of societal capacity to respond to disaster at that location. Holding risk constant, vulnerability increases when society lacks the capacity to counter the effects of disaster. Therefore, institutions and social structures that can reduce disaster risks—through effective preparedness, response, or recovery—matter significantly in diminishing vulnerability.

Consistent with a major thrust of the Hyogo and Sendai frameworks, the authors of this volume, seeing a major opportunity, emphasize the development and enhancement of local capacities for disaster risk management. That focus is essential to redress the imbalance that Hyogo and Sendai highlighted: dependence on the role of national and provincial governments or the international community. In the past, because those institutions had low confidence in or distrusted local capacity to handle disasters, they frequently took too few steps to encourage or develop it. Trust will come with demonstrated local capacity and competence, but those capabilities have to be not only built by the localities themselves but also nurtured by higher level governments and national and international NGOs willing to invest time, resources, and technical assistance to build capacity.

Greater emphasis on local capacity building promises important benefits in enhancing disaster risk management. The ability to identify—and then eliminate or mitigate—risks begins with local people who are physically closest to the sources of vulnerability, have knowledge of local context that outsiders often lack, and are likely highly motivated to act against risks that threaten their families, homes, communities, and livelihoods.

Not surprisingly, *individuals and families* form the first line of preparedness. Helping them change their mindset from potential victims to proactive protectors of their families' lives and property is a critical step toward self-reliance. If educated about risk reduction, motivated, and mobilized, they can take important steps to ready themselves and those close to them for potential disaster events. As an author in this volume emphasizes, women are a potentially crucial—but previously underutilized—resource in disaster risk reduction and preparedness. Moreover, individuals and family members are frequently the true "first responders" in the event of actual crisis—for example, rescuing themselves and their loved ones from flood or landslide. That ability may be critical. If disaster occurs, help may take considerable time to arrive.

Beyond the family, *civil society* is crucial to societal resilience; it can be a major player in risk reduction and frequently plays major roles both in disaster response and during the extended period of recovery. Where social capital is bountiful, bottom up participation is a powerful way of reducing and managing disaster risks. To the extent that local communities have formal or informal groupings based on family ties, religion, neighborhood, political loyalties, avocations, work, or other forms of social capital, they have associational resources that potentially can mobilize—wholly or in part—for disaster preparedness, response, and recovery.

Local government institutions are also critical resources for grassroots risk reduction. All but the smallest communities have locally based capacity—for example, police officers and volunteer firefighters—that can serve well to meet serious emergencies. Local governments can also support civil society in mobilizing and creating social networks for risk reduction and disaster management. They also can develop operational capacity for mitigation, preparedness, and response and secure financial and technical support from external sources. However, local government can be a roadblock to disaster risk management if it does *not* make preparedness a sufficient priority; develop internal capacity for responding to extreme events, not just routine ones; reach out and network with civil society groups; and establish operational linkages with disaster resources at higher levels of government and in nonlocal civil society organizations.

As important as local mobilization is in disaster risk management, local society and institutions have insufficient capacity for dealing with the threat or actuality of very large disaster events. Mitigating or preparing to combat such events often requires financial, personnel, and technical resources well beyond the capacities of localities. One form of help involves expertise, training, and technology. For example, communities can be taught to build seismically resistant structures that can reduce casualties from earthquakes; technology can produce early warnings and convey information during disasters.

Because the impacts of actual large-scale events spill across the boundaries of local jurisdictions, they require coordinated external response in addition to local action; the severity of such events often necessitates surging people and equipment to the scene from nearby or even distant locations. National governments must supply emergency responders, equipment, and relief supplies when major disasters disable or swell beyond the capacity of local or provincial institutions to cope with the consequences. National governments may also need to serve as intermediaries between local people and institutions, on the one hand, and international humanitarian responders, on the other.

Effective integration of outside resources with local capacity is thus a major challenge of preparing for and responding to large-scale emergencies. Ideally, if disaster occurs, outside responders with superior resources will be able to couple together with local responders who can exploit their superior contextual knowledge. But when a disaster largely or totally disables local capacity, making successful integration infeasible, the effectiveness of outside response is likely to be diminished.

Nonetheless, that outside capacity from higher levels of government and national and international NGOs is crucial for adequate response even if local capacity has been disabled. Although it may prove harder for external aid givers to operate without guidance and support from local institutions, help for injured, grieving, or displaced residents is essential in a large-scale event.

In preparing for sweeping disasters, the pre-disaster creation and sustainment of linkages between levels of government is essential, as is the development of common operational frameworks that allow for coordinated action. Those frameworks are largely lacking in many places. National governments therefore should work to create such systems of coordination, disseminate them widely, and ensure that they are regularly practiced so as to increase the likelihood that effective coordination of responders from diverse locations will prove feasible in a major disaster.

Building capacity for disaster risk management, however, is politically problematic even in relatively wealthy countries and particularly challenging in developing countries like those in South Asia. These nations face extremely difficult choices in allocating scarce public resources. There is immediate and compelling need for funding education, health care, housing, economic development, among others. Disaster events, by contrast, may never occur in a particular place or in a period salient to current officials. Decision makers may thus see disaster risk reduction and preparedness as luxuries by comparison with other social investments. There are no easy answers to these hard choices. On the one hand, other needs are obvious and pressing; on the other, disasters can devastate a community or region, negating hard-won improvements and setting development back by a decade or more. The politics and economics of dealing with low-probability but very high-consequence events like natural disasters or other crises are very difficult. As Hyogo and Sendai dramatize, however, the balance must shift more in the direction of risk reduction and management.

Building Resilience

The Sendai framework captures a growing awareness among both practitioners and scholars of disaster management that our goal must be creating communities and societies that are resilient in the face of disaster. Resilience has been variously defined, but the essence of the concept is the capacity of an individual, organization, or community to adapt effectively to significant changes in its environment. Although adaptation may entail the restoration of conditions to their pre-disturbance state, it more frequently entails sustainable adjustment to a new reality.

Severe disasters demand extraordinary resilience. As my colleague Herman B. "Dutch" Leonard and I have argued elsewhere (Leonard and Howitt 2010) building resilience for such events requires a comprehensive framework for risk management. That framework highlights five elements occurring during three time frames—before, during, and after a disaster. Resilience results from effective action in each element and time frame.

In advance of a disaster: *Prevention and mitigation* efforts identify and target risks, seeking either to avert them by actions to reduce the probability that they will occur or to minimize the magnitude of damage they might otherwise cause if they do occur. As an author in this volume relates, systematic analysis of risks, drawing on disaster management and climate change science, is crucial. For example, physical vulnerabilities can be identified and removed or housing and other structures reinforced; steps to reduce the life-safety dangers of flooding can also be undertaken. Individuals and families can be empowered through education about how to protect themselves from likely dangers. One author points to the careful attention given to disaster risk management in antipoverty programming in Bangladesh.

In the same pre-disaster time frame, *response capacity* can be strengthened or put in place locally. Police and firefighters, for example, can be readied to perform disaster response work more effectively. In addition, together with local authorities, civil society organizations and whole communities can prepare for likely disaster events. Where available, they can take advantage of technical assistance and resource support from higher levels of government or national or international civil society organizations to enhance their readiness. Organizing and training volunteers for action if disaster strikes can provide critical response resources if aid from outside is delayed.

A final form of pre-disaster preparedness is *advance recovery*. That idea may seem counterintuitive. How can a society plan for recovery *before* it knows where, when, and how a disaster has occurred? However, especially for areas where specific kinds of disasters are extremely likely, government should be motivated to take steps that could make the inevitable recovery process faster, less expensive, or more complete than it would be in the absence of such preparation. While advance recovery planning could be undertaken by localities, it is more likely to occur at higher levels of government. Serious forethought can be given to what new institutions would be required for major recovery efforts, how recovery could be financed, how aid from international sources could be channeled and overseen, and how local authorities and civil society could be empowered for the multiple tasks of recovery. Advance recovery planning cannot precisely anticipate what will be needed in the aftermath of disaster. But thinking through the issues, provisionally planning for necessary resources, and putting recovery on the political agenda before a disaster actually occurs, can equip communities and countries for the massive tasks of recovery far better than would be the case if none of that planning had been done ahead of time.

During a disaster: The second time frame of risk management involves actual response during and immediately after a disaster. As the Sendai framework holds and the authors in this volume emphasize, improvement requires increased localization and attention to the most vulnerable groups in society; it entails strengthening the disaster response capacities of individuals, families, local government, and local civil society. As important as this is, though, large-scale disasters require more than local action—thus the importance of continuing to build response capacity of higher levels of government and national and international aid givers. As discussed above, moreover, improving the ability of external aid givers to couple effectively with local ones is also a significant objective.

After a disaster: Recovery after a serious disaster is an arduous process—a crucial test of societal resilience. Coping with physical destruction may be the most obvious need: clearing rubble; providing shelter and replacing housing; restoring infrastructure like roads, power lines, and water systems; and resuming basic services like garbage collection, health care, policing, and education. These tasks potentially consume substantial resources, whether provided by private individuals' savings and sweat equity or undertaken or subsidized by government or civil society organizations, but rarely are the funds and other resources available sufficient to enable speedy or full recovery. In South Asia, the balance between private and public recovery resources is usually tilted heavily toward the private, thus exacerbating the multiple social inequalities that often created disaster vulnerability in the first place.

Another critical recovery need is, as one author argues in this volume, ministering effectively to less visible but perhaps even more difficult psychological traumas, including grieving after loss of loved ones, friends, home, livelihood, or familiar life; recurring terror at what was experienced or heard about; and survivors' guilt. Frequently overlooked, responders as well as survivors may experience severe posttrauma stress.

External aid from international organizations or NGOs typically comes with strings attached—conditions on how it should be applied, managed, and accounted for—which may create perceived challenges to national sovereignty or violations of cultural norms.

Institutional innovation is often required to cope with the increased and unfamiliar demands that recovery imposes on government. Major disasters frequently lead to the establishment of new agencies (or to significant changes in existing ones) to consolidate the authority, expertise, and resources necessary to undertake the varied tasks of recovery. These include raising funds from government or external aid providers, mediating community disputes about how recovery should be conducted, overseeing or contracting for major public works projects, and managing the provision of subsidies or support to individual survivors. Recovery agencies must also manage complex accountability relationships with survivors, diverse local and external stakeholders, government agencies at different levels with overlapping responsibilities, and the international agencies and NGOs that may provide disaster aid.

Taken together, effective action against disaster in the three periods outlined above can be thought of as leverage points for enhancing societal resilience. Disaster risk management, at its heart, requires a continuous process to identify and mitigate risks, prepare to respond to the inevitable disasters that occur, and ready individuals, communities, and agencies for the tasks of recovery and reconstruction. If priorities are established and if these steps of preparedness are taken, then response to and recovery from actual disasters will be far better—and society more resilient.

Conclusion

The chapters in this volume depict many of the rich problems and challenges of creating disaster resilient communities and countries in South Asia. As the authors note, most of these countries are far better positioned to handle such disasters than they were a generation ago, but, as the authors here also demonstrate, there is still much improvement possible—and looming challenges from demographic and climate change, urbanization, migration, and social inequalities. Research like that in this volume can alert the public and policy makers to the need for better disaster risk management, help set the agenda, and generate productive debate. We need that debate—and action—going forward.

Reference

"Dutch" Leonard, H.B., and A.M. Howitt. 2010. "Acting in Time Against Disasters: A Comprehensive Risk Management Framework," In *Learning from Catastrophes: Strategies of Reaction and Response*, eds. H. Kunreuther and M. Useem, 18–40. Upper Saddle River, NJ: Wharton School Publishing/Pearson Education.

Author's Biography

Arnold M. Howitt is a faculty codirector of the Program on Crisis Leadership, as well as senior adviser of the Ash Center for Democratic Governance and Innovation, at the John F. Kennedy School of Government (HKS), Harvard University, Cambridge, MA, USA. During the 2018–19 academic year, he serves as the Johnson and Johnson Chair Professor of Leadership at Schwarzman College, Tsinghua University, Beijing, China.

Among other writings, Dr. Howitt is the coauthor/editor of *Public Health Preparedness* (2017), *Natural Disaster Management in the Asia-Pacific: Policy and Governance* (2015), *Managing Crises: Responding to Large-Scale Emergencies* (2009), *Countering Terrorism: Dimensions of Preparedness* (2003), *Perspectives on Management Capacity Building* (1986), and *Managing Federalism: Studies in Intergovernmental Relations* (1984).

Dr. Howitt earned his BA from Columbia University and his MA and PhD in political science from Harvard University.

List of Reviewers

Prof. Namrata Agrawal (National Institute of Financial Management, India)

Mr. Md Zahir Ahmed (Policy Research Centre bd, Bangladesh)

Dr. Misa Aoki (Nara Women's University, Japan)

Senior Prof. R. Lalitha S. Fernando (University of Sri Jayewardenepura, Nugegoda, Sri Lanka)

Dr. Huong Ha (Singapore University of Social Sciences, Singapore).

Ms. Nahian Nabila Hoque (Legal Council in Bangladesh)

Dr. Shafiq Islam (CRP, Savar, Dhaka, Bangladesh)

Dr. Jak Jabes (Independent Researcher, Canada)

Prof. Dr. Neena Joseph (Independent Researcher, India)

Prof. Kalpana Kharad (K.J. Somaiya College of Education, India)

Prof. Dr. Sarfraz Khawaja (Civil Services Academy, Lahore, Pakistan)

Prof. Dr. Sanjeev Kumar Mahajan (Himachal Pradesh University, India)

Prof. Dr. Steven Leibo (Russell Sage College, USA)

Mr. Himanshu Shekhar Mishra (New Delhi Television, India)

A/Prof. Md Nurul Momen (University of Rajshahi, Bangladesh)

A/Prof. Dr. Isaias S. Sealza (Xavier University, Philippines)

Dr. Olivia Tan Swee Leng (Multimedia University, Malaysia)

Dr. Stanley Bruce Thomson (Federation Business School at Federation University, Australia)

Acknowledgments

The editors take pride in acknowledging the role of the *Network of Asia Pacific Schools and Institutes of Public Administration and Governance,* popularly known by the acronym NAPSIPAG, in making the present book possible. NAPSIPAG is the largest governance research network in the Asia Pacific region, which has been regularly organizing an international meeting of administrators, academia, and nonstate bodies every year where regional scholars critically deliberate with international governance experts. This is the process through which many young and upcoming scholars are also trained and academic brilliance generated. NAPSIPAG has also helped the international policy organizations to have a better understanding of the region through a local lens of Asiatic anthropology, ethnography, and culture of administration. The book is an outcome of the academic and practitioners' discourses generated mainly by NAPSIPAG members.

It was impossible for this book to be completed without the support of members, the reviewers, the authors, family members, and friends. The editors take pride in acknowledging the great role of the reviewers and the authors. The editor wishes to thank (i) the reviewers for their professional and constructive feedback, which is valuable to the authors; (ii) the contributing authors for their cooperation during the revision stages; and (iii) Dr. Stanley Bruce Thomson for his exceptional and tireless support during the review and proofreading processes. Finally, the editors are very grateful for the advice and assistance from the series editor/s of BEP, USA.

Dr. Huong Ha
Prof. R. Lalitha S. Fernando
Prof. Sanjeev Kumar Mahajan

CHAPTER 1

Disaster Risk Management

Case Studies in South Asia— An Introduction

Huong Ha

School of Business, Singapore University of Singapore, Singapore

R. Lalitha S. Fernando

Department of Public Administration, University of Sri Jayewardenepura, Nugegoda, Sri Lanka

Sanjeev Kumar Mahajan

Himachal Pradesh University, Shimla, India

Introduction

Disasters are "frequent affairs" of any country, and they are unavoidable and non-negotiable. Thus, disaster risk management (DRM) is an ongoing, challenging and multidimensional process that requires continuous attention, effort, and resources. Effective systems and strategies are necessary in mitigating disaster risks.

The latest statistics pertaining to natural disasters in South Asia show an increasing number of casualties and physical damage. According to Guha-Sapir et al. (2016), there are four types of natural disasters, namely meteorological disasters, hydrological disasters, geophysical disasters and climatological disasters, and the total number of natural disasters in 2016 was 342 in South Asia. Although one of the Sustainable Development Goals (SDGs) focuses on strengthening resilience to respond to climate-related hazards and disasters, the outcomes of the current measures to prepare for and mitigate disaster risks are not satisfactory (Hoffmann and Muttarak 2017). Two South Asian countries (Bangladesh and Pakistan) are in the list of the top 10 countries that have been affected by climate-related risk (Kreft et al. 2016). This raises the question of "How can disasters be better managed? And how can risks be better mitigated?" given the resource constraints. Hence, this volume endeavors to provide insights into DRM in different contexts in some South Asian countries. Different countries have tried to adopt various approaches, new and old, to prepare for and manage disaster risks. Yet, the negative effects and damage caused by such disasters have not been contained. It is imperative to search for novel approaches to prepare for, manage, and mitigate disaster impacts at all levels. Thus, this edited volume aims to examine (i) the effects of different types of disaster risks, (ii) how different disaster risk and related issues have been managed, and (iii) different approaches adopted by countries to mitigate and prepare for disaster risk in the context of South Asia.

The 10 chapters, excluding the Introduction and the Conclusion chapters, covered in this volume were contributed by researchers, academics, and industry practitioners from different countries in South Asia from various disciplines and interests. This has enriched the depth and the breadth of the discussion. The uniqueness of this volume is the focus on special topics, such as nuclear disasters, e-waste disasters, psychological factors, medicinal plants in disasters that have been rarely discussed in the literature.

Issues and Challenges Associated with Disaster Risk in the Context of South Asian Countries

South Asia, in the twenty-first century, continues to be afflicted by a variety of natural disasters. The frequency and intensity of natural disasters has significantly increased in the last decade. The fact that 481 disaster-related events occurred during 2005 through 2015 in South Asia claiming about 135,000 lives leading to economic losses underlines the issue at hand (Bhatt et al. 2017). The extreme weather events along with un-planned human settlements, unsafe building practices, high population densities across South Asian countries, etc. have compounded and aggravated the effects of natural and man-made disasters in the recent time leading to vulnerability of people at large.

Apart from this, the damage resulting from natural disasters have strained the development opportunities because the loss of infrastructure results in increased pressure on the economy. Evidence has been reported that natural disasters have caused the death of thousands of civilians, loss of and damage to assets, breakdown of businesses, and interruption of the development process for income-generating activities and ending people's livelihoods, and so forth (Dominguez et al. 2018; Sanderson and Sharma 2016). Despite all the debates, discussions, and statistics related to disaster risks and events, the focus on people is still not adequately established, leaving them displaced and in utter poverty. Sustainable and inclusive development is a failure in disaster-stricken areas, and impact the affected victims and their families.

Though disaster risk in the South Asia region has increased, the level of understanding and awareness of disaster risk seems low. Exposure, and vulnerability to natural hazards and their consequential impact, are not yet at the forefront of development agendas (World Bank 2012). Hence, to facilitate disaster preparedness, one critical need is better access to robust and accurate data on disaster risks. Developing a comprehensive database at the South Asia and regional and country level will help countries have long-term planning and capacity building to make better decisions to mitigate the effects of natural disasters. Thus, this volume endeavors to provide insights into issues associated with DRM in South Asian countries.

An Overview of the Chapters

This edited volume starts with a chapter focusing on the practices of countries in South Asia with regard to disaster risk reduction and adaptation strategies (Chapter 2) by Dr. Md Nurul Momen. The main purpose of disaster risk reduction (DRR) is to mitigate the damages and losses caused by natural disasters. The author explains that the process of DRM should be people centric and inclusive, that is, involving local communities and vulnerable groups. Also, some countries may have more experience in managing and preparing for disasters; whereas other countries may have less experience. Thus, sharing experience and good practices would help countries improve the effectiveness of their DRM strategies. Also, any initiatives to prepare for disaster risks, disaster mitigation, and recovery should address the issues associated with social inequalities and vulnerabilities of people who are the regular victims of disasters on a regular basis (World Bank 2009). Finally, local communities should be engaged as strategic partners in the disaster management process (FEMA 2011). Thus, DRR is possible if one could prevent causal factors of disasters. Reducing exposure to hazards, lessening vulnerability of people and property, wise management of land and the environment, and improving preparedness and early warning for adverse events are all examples of DRR (UNISDR, n.d.).

Professor Mahfuzul Haque in Chapter 3 suggests that local communities are key beneficiaries and contributors to the DRM process. Thus, a bottom-up approach should be adopted, instead of the traditional top-down approach, to prepare for disasters and mitigate damages during and after disasters. Some best practices are observed from a comparative analysis of the four major cyclones in Bangladesh. They include (i) a paradigm shift from relief and rehabilitation to risk reduction would help to mitigate damages by disasters, (ii) an early warning at the community level would be more effective than late warning, (iii) community empowerment and building community resilience is an important task. Such best practices have contributed to reducing risk factors and loss of lives (Gero, Meheux, and Dominey-Howes 2011; Ha 2014, 2017; Ha, Fernando, and Mahmood 2015a, 2015b. In the process of DRR, communication and coordination among stakeholders including citizens are of paramount importance.

Chapter 4 discusses an interesting topic, that is, psychological impacts of disasters. Dr. Evelyn Gay explains that not only survivors of disasters, but also their family members, social workers, and other stakeholders are mentally affected by disasters in some ways (Sajid 2007). Marcelo et al. (2018) proposed a model to explain four types of psychosocial impact: resilient, traumatic, sensitive, and witness. The authors noted that people are more prone to illness when they are exposed to a disaster, and less when they are protected. Gay proposes that psychological support and counselling to people who are affected by disasters can help to mitigate the adverse effect after disasters. Such support includes informal social support networks via social media, or small support groups in the community, formal support by local and state governments, and civil society organizations (Juvva and Rajendran 2000). It is also important to have screening to detect post-traumatic stress disorder symptoms, and provide sufferers with social support, mental health, and counselling services (Sajid 2007). In a nutshell, both physical and psychology damages by natural disasters should be mitigated by different channels.

In Chapter 5, Professor Neena Joseph explains how women in India have been affected by disasters. Also, women can play an important role in the process of DRR by contributing various ways; namely, protect their children's safety, prevent them from diseases and ensure family members', particularly children's, health and nutrition. This chapter also explores alternatives for DRR, for example, adoption of Gj/cPW technology. Overall, technology can enhance the income of local women, and thus can also be considered the future of DRR (Mu 2016). The findings suggest that women should be engaged in the DRR and DRM processes in order to be able to contribute to solving disaster-related problems, and also reduce their vulnerability during and after disasters (Nasreen 2012). Women should be empowered and well-equipped with information, knowledge, and skills to deal with disaster-related issues within their capacities (Ha, Fernando, and Mahmood 2015a, 2015b).

Similarly to Chapter 5, Associate Professor Marzina Begum, in Chapter 6 also focuses on the impacts of climate change as a contributor to disaster risk on women's health in Bangladesh. The UN Women Fiji Multi-Country Office (n.d.) reported that women and children are more likely to die or be injured in a disaster 14 times more than men. Disasters, including climate change, have affected women's health in different forms, such as miscarriage, mental and physical health risks, maternal mortality risk, hypertension, and more (Rahman 2008). Thus, Begum argues that governments should focus on building women's capability to respond to disaster risks and vulnerabilities. Women should not be marginalized in the society, especially in Bangladesh. Hence, women should be engaged in disaster risk preparation and mitigation processes, as well as climate change adaptation strategies and initiatives (Nasreen 2012). Finally, community participation is too important to be ignored because it plays an important part in the battle against climate change incidents, which relate to health risks and vulnerabilities in Bangladesh (Ha and Ahmad 2014). Sohrabizadeh, Tourani, and Khankeh (2016) noted that the impact of disasters on the lives of women is different from other groups in a community and women's fundamental rights to health and safety are often violated after disasters.

Another interesting topic, e-waste (electronic-waste) in the context of Bangladesh, is covered in Chapter 7. E-waste has been considered as a hazardous substance. It is noted that developed countries are the sources of e-waste, which are exported to developing countries (Breivik, Armitage, and Jones 2014; Perkins et al. 2014). These developing countries become a dumping ground of e-waste, creating not only an environmentally hazardous situation but also one that is hazardous to human welfare in Bangladesh. However, Nahian Nabila Hoque observed that there has been no particular law or regulation to deal with e-waste in the country. However, the government is introducing rules to manage e-waste because the current state of e-waste handling does not contribute to reducing environmental concerns (Environment and Social Development Organization 2014). As per World Health Organization (2018) recycling of valuable elements contained in e-waste, such as copper and gold, has become a source of income in mostly the informal sector of developing or emerging industrialized countries. However, primitive recycling techniques, such as burning cables to retain the copper, expose both adult and child workers as well as their families to a range of hazardous substances. Thus, new approaches, including the adoption of advanced technology to manage e-waste may improve the country's resilience toward risk (Lundgren 2012; Tanskanen 2013).

Associate Professor Vinay Sharma, Pramod Chandra and Associate Professor Rajat Agrawal in Chapter 8, approach disasters from another dimension, that is, how residents' livelihood based on medicinal and aromatic plants is affected by disasters in Uttarakhand, India. This part of the country has a history of producing a significant amount of medicinal and aromatic plants that can treat human and livestock sicknesses (Bisht, Negi, and Bhandari 2016). Thus, they are one of the main sources of the livelihood for the residents (Chauhan 2010; Lesk, Rowhani, and Ramankutty 2016; Sati 2013). Yet, this area has also been prone to disasters that do affect the residents in many ways, such as the loss of biodiversity, natural resources, and the loss of high-value species as well as medicinal and aromatic plants (Kala 2014). This chapter examines the impact of natural disasters on the development and sustainability of medicinal and aromatic plants, which, in turn, affects the socioeconomic development and ecosystem in the area (Kala 2014). Many governance-related aspects emerge as sources of problems for the local residents. For instance, the unclear role of various institutions engaged in the management of local resources, and the lack of information during and after disasters. The chapter proposes a framework that can help respond to disasters to sustain the livelihood of local residents via sustainable development of medicinal and aromatic plants. This framework includes four main elements: (i) land use planning, that is, buffer plantations in the barren land should be available for the cultivation of medicinal and aromatic plants in order to improve the production and create alternative spaces of the livelihood for local residents (Gautam and Anderson 2016); (ii) existing habitats of the medicinal and aromatic plants should be conserved and developed; (iii) sufficient information should be available to various stakeholders who are involved in the development of medicinal and aromatic plants; and (iv) the parties involved should adopt advanced information technology tools to enhance the awareness of local residents about the adverse effects of disasters on the local resources and the livelihood of local residents so that they are motivated to contribute to sustainable initiatives (Mu 2016; Sharma, Joshi, and Agrawal 2015).

Chapter 9, by Md Zahir Ahmed, Professor Akbaruddin Ahmad and Dr. Oli Ahmad, focuses on a rare topic, that is, an assessment of whether the content of how to prepare for disasters in high school textbooks in Bangladesh is sufficient for students. As proposed by the authors, DRM and climate change being incorporated in the content of academic curricula at school is a good start to educate young people about risks and prepare them for responding to such risks. Lessons on climate change and disaster risk provide students with an overview of the causes and consequences of climate change and how to prepare and respond to disasters.

However, the content of such lessons may not be sufficient to entice students' interest and understanding. Thus, this chapter examines to what extent practical knowledge on climate change and disasters is included in the textbooks used in high schools in Bangladesh. The findings suggest that there is a deviation with regard to knowledge of disaster management from the textbook among high school students in the rural and urban areas in Bangladesh.

The last chapter, Chapter 10, by Prof. Sarfraz Khawaja, Dr. Ha and Ayesha Akbar, discusses how technology can improve the effectiveness of disaster management in Pakistan. Adoption of IT in education and health can contribute to prepare for disasters and mitigate the impact of disasters.

Key Lessons

Natural disasters are extreme occurrences in nature. People in many countries are not prepared to respond to risk and face the consequences of disasters. Disasters disrupt the normal course of life in the affected area for communities and the countries. This often results in the halt of economic and developmental activities. It is evident from the outcomes of the chapters that economic and human losses associated with each disaster are on the rise. However, natural disasters cannot be prevented but the stress is to reduce the underlying factors of risk, prepare and initiate an immediate response in case of disaster.

DRM is a process of managing and coordinating activities and responses, resources, and stakeholders-- pre-disaster, during, and post-disaster. Many agencies such as the United Nations, Food and Agriculture Organization (USA), the World Bank and agencies at the national, regional and local levels are searching for new and novel approaches to mitigate the effects of disasters. Policies regarding mitigation, preparedness measures for the vulnerability reduction and professional response to disasters have been made; yet their implementation may not produce the desirable outcomes. Evidence shows that there is a gap between mitigation, preparedness, and responses to disasters and three attributes, namely the set goals and objectives, the course of action, and the values inherent in the policy (Sanderson and Sharma 2016).

It is difficult to identify why a policy does not work. Usually the fault finding is rendered at the implementation level while the problem might lie in its formulation. This can happen due to a disconnect with the problems at the local or the grassroots level. Throughout the chapters it has been observed that the policies are well formulated, but in their implementation there is lack of operational sources, trained personnel, or empathy.

Formulation of policies in a country is for the advancement of its people. Therefore, it is important that the periodic monitoring and evaluation of policies should be carried out by the concerned agencies. Policy evaluation process/es should be consistent and continuous activities to ratify the policies by data analysis. The world needs to learn these key lessons to mitigate the effects of disasters.

Conclusion

This chapter has discussed the issues and challenges associated with DRM. Countries around the world have strived hard to prepare for and respond to disasters. Nevertheless, many factors, such as governance framework, resources, approaches, etc., affect their efforts, and make the disaster risk process more challenging.

One of the key lessons, learned from the chapters in this volume, is the shift of the focus from a reactive approach to a more proactive approach in DRM. Preparation for and mitigation to disaster risk would contribute to reducing the adverse effect of disasters. A proactive approach in DRM also allows implementers to have sufficient time to engage stakeholders, and to mobilize and allocate resources efficiently. In addition, it also enables different sectors and actors to prepare the vulnerable groups, including women, children, the disabled, the elderly, for disasters via training and education. There is an interdependence among activities, for example, initiatives to achieve SDGs would, in turn, contribute to address the issues associated with disaster risk and climate change management. Thus, it is difficult to draw a clear line between DRM, climate change management, and development for SDGs. This suggests that discussion and solutions for these three dimensions must be addressed simultaneously at all levels.

References

Bhatt, M. R., K. K. Durrani, B. Wisner, A. Bhatti, M. Taher, and K. Fernando. 2017. *South Asia Disaster Report 2016*. Colombo, Sri Lanka: Duryog Nivaran Secretariat. https://www.preventionweb.net /publications/view/52877

Bisht, V. K., J. S. Negi, and A. K. Bhandari. 2016. "Check on Extinction of Medicinal Herbs in Uttarakhand: No Need to Uproot." *National Academy Science Letters* 39, no. 3, pp. 233–35.

Breivik, J. M., F. W. Armitage, and K. C. Jones. 2014. "Tracking the Global Generation and Exports of E-waste: Do Existing Estimates Add Up?" *Environmental Science and Technology* 48, no. 15, pp. 8735–43.

Chauhan, R. S. 2010. "Socioeconomic Improvement through Medicinal and Aromatic Plants (MAPs) Cultivation in Uttarakhand, India." *Journal of Sustainable Agriculture* 34, no. 6, pp. 647–58.

Dominguez, F., S. Dall'Erba, S. Huang, A. Avelino, A. Mehran, H. Hu, A. Schmidt, L. Schick, and D. Lettenmaier. 2018. "Tracking an Atmospheric River in a Warmer Climate: From Water Vapour to Economic Impacts." *Earth System Dynamics* 9, no. 1, pp. 249–66. doi:10.5194/ esd-9-249-2018

Environment and Social Development Organization. 2014. *Magnitude of the Flow of E-waste in Bangladesh*. Dhaka, Bangladesh: Environment and Social Development Organization.

FEMA. 2011. *A Whole Community Approach to Emergency Management: Principles, Themes, and Pathways for Action FDOC 104-008-1/December 2011*. Washington, DC: US Department of Homeland Security.

Gautam, Y., and P. Andersen. April, 2016. "Rural Livelihood Diversification and Household Well-being: Insights from Humla, Nepal." *Journal of Rural Studies* 44, pp. 239–49.

Gero, A., K. Meheux, and D. Dominey-Howes. 2011. "Integrated Community Based Disaster Risk Reduction and Climate Change Adaptation: Examples from the Pacific." *Natural Hazards and Earth System Sciences* 11, pp. 101–13.

Guha-Sapir, D., P. Hoyois, P. Wallemacq, and R. Below. 2016. *Annual Disaster Statistical Review 2016: The Numbers and Trends*. Brussel, Belgium: Centre for Research on the Epidemiology of Disasters

(CRED), Institute of Health and Society (IRSS) University catholique de Louvain.

Ha, H. 2014. "Land Use and Disaster Governance in Asia: An Introduction." In *Land and Disaster Management Strategies in Asia,* ed. H. Ha, pp. 1–14. New Delhi, India: Springer.

Ha, H. 2017. *Risk Governance and Disaster Impacts in Asia.* PreventionWeb, UN Office for Disaster Risk Reduction. http://www.preventionweb.net/experts/oped/view/55397

Ha, H., and A. Ahmad. 2014. "Bangladesh: Natural Disaster Risk Management." In *Land and Disaster Management Strategies in Asia,* ed. H. Ha, pp. 83–98. New Delhi, India: Springer.

Ha, H., L. Fernando, and A. Mahmood. 2015a. "Disaster Management in Asia: Lessons Learned and Policy Implications." In *Strategic Disaster Risk Management in Asia,* eds. H. Ha, L. Fernando and A. Mahmood, pp. 221–26. New Delhi, India: Springer.

Ha, H., L. Fernando, and A. Mahmood. 2015b. "Strategic Disaster Risk Management in Asia: An Introduction." In *Strategic Disaster Risk Management in Asia,* eds. H. Ha, L. Fernando, and A. Mahmood, pp. 1–13. New Delhi, India: Springer.

Hoffmann, R., and R. Muttarak. 2017. "Learn from the Past, Prepare for the Future: Impacts of Education and Experience on Disaster Preparedness in the Philippines and Thailand." *World Development* 96, pp. 32–51.

Juvva, S., and P. Rajendran. 2000. "Disaster Mental Health: A Current Perspective." *The Indian Journal of Social Work* 61, no. 4, pp. 527–41.

Kala, C. P. 2014. "Deluge, Disaster and Development in Uttarakhand Himalayan Region of India: Challenges and Lessons for Disaster Management." *International Journal of Disaster Risk Reduction* 8, pp.143–52.

Kreft, S., D. Eckstein, L. Dorsch, and L. Fischer. 2016. *Global Climate Risk Index 2016: Who Suffers Most from Extreme Weather Events? Weather-related Loss Events in 2014 and 1995 to 2014.* Bonn, Germany: GermanWatch.

Lesk, C., P. Rowhani, and N. Ramankutty. 2016. "Influence of Extreme Weather Disasters on Global Crop Production." *Nature* 529, no. 7584, pp. 84–87.

Lundgren, K. 2012. *The Global Impact of E-waste: Addressing the Challenge*. International Labour Office, Programme of Safety and Health at Work and the Environment, Sectoral Activités Department, Geneva, ILO.

Marcelo, L., F. Ahumada, A. Araneda, and J. Botella. 2018. "What Is the Psychosocial Impact of Disasters? A Meta-Analysis." *Issues in Mental Health Nursing* 39, no. 4, pp. 320–27, doi:10.1080/01612840.2017.1393033

Mu, L. 2016. *Technology: The Future of Disaster Risk Reduction?* Geneva, Switzerland: UNISDR. https://www.unisdr.org/archive/51043

Nasreen, M. 2012. *Women and Girls: Vulnerable or Resilient?* Dhaka, Bangladesh: Institute of Disaster Management and Vulnerability Studies, Dhaka University.

Perkins, D. N., M. B. Drisse, T. Nxele, and P. D. Sly. 2014. "E-Waste: A Global Hazard." *Annals of Global Health* 80, no. 4, pp. 286–95.

Rahman, A. 2008. "Climate Change and Its Impact on Health in Bangladesh." *Regional Health Forum, Dhaka* 12, no. 1, pp. 16–26.

Sanderson, D., and A. Sharma, eds. 2016. *World Disasters Report Resilience: Saving Lives Today, Investing for Tomorrow*. Geneva, Switzerland: International Federation of Red Cross and Red Crescent Societies.

Sajid, S. M. 2007. "Unearthing the Most Vulnerable: Psychological Impact of Natural Disasters." *The European Journal of Psychiatry* 21, no. 3, pp. 230–31.

Sati, V. P. 2013. "Cultivation of Medicinal Plants and Its Contribution to Livelihood Enhancement in the Indian Central Himalayan Region." *Advancement in Medicinal Plant Research* 1, no. 2, pp. 17–23.

Sharma, V., K. K. Joshi, and R. Agrawal. 2015. "Mitigating Disasters through Community Involvement and Righteous Practices in Himalayan region of Uttarakhand, India." In *Strategic Disaster Risk Management in Asia*, eds. H. Ha, R. L. S. Fernando, and A. Mahmood, pp. 99–114. New Delhi, India: Springer.

Sohrabizadeh, S., S. Tourani, and H. R. Khankeh. 2016. "Women and Health Consequences of Natural Disasters: Challenge or Opportunity?" *Women Health* 56, no. 8, pp. 977–93. doi:10.1080/0363024 2.2016.1176101

Tanskanen, P. 2013. "Management and Recycling of Electronic Waste." *Acta Materialia* 61, no. 3, pp. 1001–11.

UN Women Fiji Multi-Country Office. n.d. *Why Is Climate Change a Gender Issue?* Fiji, Oceania: UN Women Fiji Multi-Country Office.

UNISDR. n.d. *Our Mandate.* UNISDR. https://www.unisdr.org/who-we-are/mandate (July 29, 2018 accessed).

World Health Organization. 2018. *Electronic Waste.* Geneva, Switzerland: WHO. http://www.who.int/ceh/risks/ewaste/en

World Bank. 2009. *Building Resilient Communities: Risk Management and Response to Natural Disasters through Social Funds and Community-Driven Development Programs.* Washington, DC: World Bank.

World Bank. 2012. *Disaster Risk Management in South Asia: A Regional Overview.* Washington, DC: World Bank, License: CC BY 3.0 IGO. https://openknowledge.worldbank.org/handle/10986/13218

CHAPTER 2

The Process of Disaster Management

Practices from Disaster—Affected Countries

Md Nurul Momen

Department of Public Administration, University of Rajshahi, Rajshahi, Bangladesh

Introduction

Natural disasters have profound reoccurring effects on the future direction of human life on the planet. Having reviewed the contemporary literature on natural disaster, itis found that the impact of recent disasters is very much different compared to the disasters that occurred in prehistoric times. Even after knowing the dangers of unplanned development, many states still allow some projects to operate in the disaster-prone areas, which threatens the environment and social livelihoods. For example, every year on the Indian subcontinent cyclones take place, but it is an unfortunate reality that the states of the region have many commercial development projects in the coastal areas. As a result, this had a devastating effect during the Indian Ocean earthquake and tsunami of 2004 in which 283,106 people who lost their lives (Pinkowski 2008a). On a particular note, environment and social livelihood can be saved through the concerted efforts that help to achieve the target of successful disaster management and help mitigate and reduce the potential casualties and destruction of property, or lessen the magnitude of destruction of natural resources, as humans depend on nature. To address the issues, it essentially requires proper planning and preparedness mechanisms that may help us to avoid and mitigate potential losses and other consequences of disasters.

Many national and international experts, and bodies, in regard to climate change, are quite concerned about the future impact of disasters. Therefore, the states along with other Multi-Stakeholder Partnerships (MSPs) have to take huge responsibilities to employ a better plan of action in order to save lives and property. Pinkowski (2008a) explored the devastation of the 1906 San Francisco earthquake and fire that caused 700 deaths. Thirty-five years prior, 1871, a similar level of destruction occurred when fire engulfed up to 4square miles of the center of Chicago, which resulted in the killing of hundreds of people. Despite the disaster, in both cases the states successfully developed a plan of action to reconstruct the infrastructure in both cities; however, they introduced strict regulatory frameworks. For example, introduction of improved building codes, improved construction equipment in order to encounter the possible risks of disaster, better preparedness plans for minimizing disaster losses, and obviously establishing better early warning systems (Pinkowski 2008a).

Johnson and Olshansky (2016) found that after devastating earthquakes, the government of China and New Zealand established a unit called "recovery management and policy creation." They added that after the 1995 and 2011 earthquakes, Japan strictly followed coordination among the concerned agencies at the national level, but also encouraged some decentralized functions across the different levels of government and organizations. More to the point, India, Indonesia, and the USA adopted decentralized approaches after large disasters (Johnson and Olshansky 2016). Given the nature of the objective of the chapter, it requires to solicit accounts of knowledge from some deliberately selected countries involved with the disaster management process, which presents their perspectives and shows us some lessons and opportunities to fix long-standing disaster management challenges.

Operationalization of Concepts

In general, a disaster risk may bring injuries, loss of life and damage to resources, thus it hampers social services and economic activities, and has negative impacts on the natural environment. No doubt wherever mankind lives in the global village, they are being threatened by different kinds of either natural or man-made disasters. Over the years, natural disasters have occurred with an increased level of frequency in the world, thus an impact on a greater number of loss of lives and destruction of property. Therefore, it is the responsibility of all countries to address the vulnerabilities of human beings due to consequences of disaster. When it comes to the definition of disasters, the Center for Research on the Epidemiology of Disasters (CRED) defines it as

> Situation or event, which overwhelms local capacity, necessitating a request to national or international level for external assistance; an unforeseen and often sudden event that causes great damage, destruction and human suffering. Though often caused by nature, disasters can have human origins (CRED 2007).

On a particular note, data shows the cruelty of disasters in that more than 226 million people on the planet are affected by natural disasters every year, and in 2010 alone, 373 natural disasters caused the death of 226,000 and affected the livelihood of 207,000 (Withanaarachchi and Setunge 2014). In another study conducted by the United Nations found that natural disasters caused death of more than 600,000personsand severely damaged the economy in the last two decades (Chan 2015). It is worth mentioning that 90 percent of these deaths occur in poor countries (CRED 2016) where limited resources put pressure on disaster mitigation.

An Exploration of Vulnerability

In a presentation in the sixth Conference of the Parties to the UNFCCC, Robert P. Watson, chair of the International Panel on Climate Change (IPCC), operationalizes vulnerability as the extent to which a natural or social system prone to sustaining damage from climate change (IPCC 2000). To explain it more precisely, Misomali and McEntire (2008) see the concepts from two perspectives: mapping proneness to disaster, and insufficient capability in regard to disaster preparedness. When it comes to defining proneness to disaster, IPCC and other scholars, especially

Misomali and McEntire (2008), usually relate it to one's risk or vulnerability. For example, individuals residing in the coastal areas are more prone to hazards caused by cyclone or any other forms of storm. On the other hand, another perspective of vulnerability relates to the insufficient capability that corresponds to an emergency entity's incapacity to respond to and recover from a disaster. To further explain the phenomenon, state agencies involved in disaster preparedness become vulnerable, when it is established that they lack the capacity to deal with natural disasters.

Theoretical Lenses

It is important to note that there has been a shifting in the paradigm on the approach of disaster management that is called "Risk reduction." The main argument of the said approach directs the safety and protection of people and property, thus consequently helps to the achievement of sustainable development. While the traditional approach in disaster management is mainly focused on rescue and relief efforts (Quyyum 2015), it is the duty of every government to immediately provide relief and rehabilitation assistance alongside other nongovernmental organizations and international organizations.

However, approximately 60 million people in the world today are currently displaced and/or have lost their livelihood due to many reasons, for instance, political violence, climate change, natural disasters, and economic development. Of these vulnerable people, 30 percent are supported by humanitarian aid organizations through different programs, but the remaining70 percent have to manage their own shelters. In 2015 it was estimated that shelter for displaced individuals requires 1.8 billion US dollars, but only a quarter of the amount was covered (Hendriks et al. n.d.).

No doubt, disasters make serious impacts on disaster-prone countries, which disrupt social and economic activities, and endanger the livelihood of the affected families and communities. When it is thought that a natural disaster is inevitable or going to happen, it means that it goes beyond the capacity of humans to face it. In these contexts, it requires mapping out the relationship between disasters and vulnerability. It is commonly perceived that sudden disasters that cannot be effectively handled by emergency response agencies, but its severe impacts can be significantly lessened by adopting different mechanisms of disaster risk reduction. So, meaning that natural disaster may not be prevented even in an advanced technology-based country, but a developed framework in disaster management may have an effect on lives and resources, thus less destruction. However, due to the inevitable nature of disasters, the local community accepts the danger of future disaster. Given the context, all of the countries now attempt to take some initiatives for a sustained capacity strengthening, and institutional competence of the concerned agencies and empower people to stay in local disaster-prone places. Note also that the power of resilience after a disaster among the affected communities occupies the center stage in the recent debates and discussions on disaster management.

As stated earlier, there has been a paradigmatic shift in disaster management approach (Jenkins 2015), in the past it only focused on the recovery phase after the disaster. Now, it turns into a multidimensional disaster management approach that combines different strategies, and participation of community at the local level. Furthermore, it is now increasingly realized that every stakeholder in disaster management process requires mapping out the disaster risks and consequences that help them in the fight against disasters and risks. When talking about the disaster risks, Sonny (1999) focused on some reasons of risks due to flawed development plans, which often results in occurrence of different types of disasters. More to the point, the new paradigm emphasizes not only the reasons of disaster occurrence, but also the enhanced capacity to handle and reduce the extent of future disaster risks (Medury 2008).

However, integrated disaster management strategy was introduced for the first time at a conference held on May 23 to 27, 1994 and adopted in Japan through the Yokohama Strategy and plan of action for a safer world. The said strategy and plan of action originated from within the framework called as the International Decade for Natural Disaster Risk Reduction (IDNDR). For achieving the target of vulnerability reduction, it emphasizes a sustainable solution by pointing out that "disaster prevention, mitigation, and preparedness are better than disaster response" (Medury 2008). Furthermore, there has been a recent effort in changing the disaster management approach, for instance, building the resilience power of concerned authorities and affected communities through proper diagnosis of their current status of vulnerabilities and capacities. Note also that traditional top-down approach to dealing with disasters have not shown much success in the past. This suggests the requirement of a community-based and bottom-up approach that helps to specify particular needs and strategies for disaster risks at the local level.

After 6 years of the Yokohama Strategy in 2000, the International Strategy of Disaster Reduction (ISDR) declared an objective of putting power into resilient communities in facing natural disasters. The ISDR in its declaration strongly considered the adoption of appropriate disaster risks reduction strategies in order to facilitate sustained economic growth and development. To them, these strategies and initiative can reduce the magnitude of human suffering, and lessen the impact of a disaster on the economy. For building disaster-resilient communities, active participation of vulnerable families and communities is required in every stage of the implementation strategy. The question is why do we need to strengthen the capacity of local communities? In reply, itis pointed out that local communities act as the first responders to any unanticipated dangers before seeking any other external assistance. If local communities in disaster-prone areas are conscious about the future possibility of disasters, this enables them to deal with possible threats and face them effectively. Hence, for reducing the disaster vulnerabilities of communities, different stakeholders apart from national government are required to identify and analyze the deficit of strengths and capacities of who are at risks and explore the different types of vulnerabilities among the affected community at various levels (Medury 2008).

It is important to note that there are some natural disasters that are not easy to predict such as underwater earthquakes, but through analyzing earlier data it is possible to generate an idea where they are most likely to happen. However, recently, the capacity to identify the location of future earthquakes has significantly developed, since the number of seismograph stations across the globe has been increased (350 in 1931 increased to 8,000) (Pinkowski 2008b). Furthermore, the tremendous changes in satellite images, improvement of local warning stations and measurement instruments in the last two decades have also increased the effectiveness in alerting the resident population. Thus, it helps to enhance the ability and provide quick messages to any sort of future natural disasters in coastal communities. On the other hand, academicians and experts recommend introduction of curriculum on disaster management in educational institutions, and training and awareness programs to local communities in disaster-prone areas is another lesson learned from many case studies. This helps to train affected people in the appropriate behavior indifferent forms of storms, as well as increasing knowledge on warning signs. The disaster awareness activities and new curricula in educational institutions is a continuous process and guided by a sound disaster management policy, laws and regulations, and also importantly, requires sufficient resources to execute the strategy and plan of action.

On the other hand, for a sound disaster management practice, no weak housing can be sustainable in the extreme force from a powerful natural disaster, so a well-designed strong infrastructure can provide shelter to affected communities. Given the context, it is suggested that public infrastructure should serve multiple uses including serving as shelters to the affected communities, or as a storage point of disaster relief and supplies, and even can be used as an information center for the local communities. Hence, public infrastructure in the disaster-prone areas requires strict building codes so that it can survive even in severe disaster conditions. Furthermore, the so-called development approaches in the coastal areas endangers the natural resources and livelihood. For instance, destruction of mangrove forests due to port development that put the coastal residents at greater risks from different kinds of storms. Therefore, it is suggested that coastal restoration projects would be invaluable to protect against tidal surges. For doing so, environment requires replanting mangrove forests, and banning any projects from further destruction of natural resources (Pinkowski 2008b).

Disaster Management Practices in the Global Perspectives

Vulnerability occurs due to many factors such as demographic patterns (for instance, poverty, growing population) that have contributed to vulnerability in disasters. Note also that other factors such as lack of emergency preparedness and weak emergency management institutions, and incapacity of local communities also trigger vulnerability in disasters.

Emergency Preparedness

Absence of emergency preparedness is a frequent policy failure that has been experienced across the globe, and even in technologically advanced countries. Misomali and McEntire (2008) found that in Malawi, heavy rainfalls cause flooding, as a consequence, people suffered a lot in the monsoon period. As a part of the responsibility, the government of Malawi had not been successful in institutionalizing a better disaster preparedness system before the incident that could have minimized human suffering or that could have adequately prepared for imminent flood conditions. It is not only the case of Malawi, in most cases the government reacts after the flooding, but human loss and suffering has already been observed. It is argued that a reactive approach in disaster management always fails to reduce the vulnerability of people and loss of property. Failure in emergency preparedness is also observed even to the countries where science and technology has reached advanced levels. For example, in the case of Hurricane Katrina 2005, the city of New Orleans government faced an experience that never occurred to them in the recent past; therefore, they had not taken emergency preparedness to the level of being hit with a massive and record-breaking strength of hurricane (Misomali and McEntire 2008).

On the other hand, an important cornerstone of emergency preparedness begins with an access to local healthcare institutions of each country. In this process, there is an importance of improved health sectoring in terms of health care services and quality of health care to all affected patients during the disaster event it may face. Although it is being claimed by health care institutions that tremendous improvements have taken place in their services, hospital preparedness for the local community is still far from the reality after a catastrophic event (Powers 2008). For example, it has been reported that the hurricanes of Katrina, Wilma, and Rita; in the Northeast caused widespread power outages and the man-made disaster of 9/11 presented a bad experience to healthcare services and challenged the US healthcare system for emergency preparedness during disasters (Cagliuso et al. 2008).

However, emergency management in the United States covers four important aspects: disaster preparedness, disaster response, organizing recovery, and disaster mitigation. These phases are considered as a cycle and interrelated, as one phase actually moves to the next (Cutter and Gall 2006). Under emergency conditions, it is essentially required to achieve the ability to deliver all needed emergency support in the affected areas in due time. Experience has shown that in the developing countries re-sources are scarce initially for disaster response. However, in many cases of storms, drinking water and other supplies may arrive days to weeks later, when the local community is beginning to recover based on supplies from other sources. In some cases, a further complication is where necessary instruments are held up in transportation (waste) and sit idle (Moeller 2008). For example, in the 2010s devastating Haitian earthquake, re-lief and recovery efforts came under fire in the media and independent research, as immediately after the disaster it failed to reach out to most affected Haitians due to logistical challenges and breakdown of the traffic control system at the Port-au-Prince airport. That condition compelled cargo aircraft to turn away, as the population became frantic. Hence, it could be said that ambiguous and chaotic relief effort costs more lives needlessly, because in the emergency situation relief workers are confused over where to take the relief aid and where to distribute it safely.

Hence, maintaining situational awareness is a key to emergency pre-paredness that assists the protection and safety of the public in manag-ing catastrophic disaster. However, situational awareness is defined as an understanding and comprehension about the current environment, and projection from a disaster (Moeller 2008), if there is any inability to com-prehend and relate situational awareness at any place that may lead to disastrous results. Therefore, it is suggested to put extra effort and sound policy into maintaining a focused situational awareness in emergency di-saster responses to help manage hazards. For instance, it is reported that mangrove forests in Thailand protected buildings from damages and re-duced significantly the causalities during the tsunami of December 2004. Sand dunes in Sri Lanka's national parks considerably lessen the quantity of seawater from penetrating inland (Pinkowski 2008b). On the other hand, the government of Bangladesh has decided to move forward with the construction of coal-based Rampal power plant near to the largest mangrove forest in the world (Sundarban); however, UNESCO and other national environment experts have already raised concerns about the pro-posed project and asked the government to reconsider it.

Building Indigenous Capacities

No doubt, all disasters are local, hence, disaster preparedness and its recovery should start with local communities. In many countries around the globe communities have their own indigenous knowledge and skills to cope with future disasters. Rural communities in many African countries face acute shortages in food production due to drought, but they have been successful in preventing famine by employing a number of strategies (Medury 2008), As a strategy, in the northern part of Ghana, young men travel to southern part during the dry season in order to find part-time employment opportunity in the cocoa-producing areas of Ashanti or the Ivory Coast. In Mozambique, in the province of Zambesia, as a specific effort during the dry season to combat food shortages, affected groups are used to changing the regular diet items, and reducing the amount of food intake (Medury 2008).

Apart from that, local communities bring and use traditional insights and age-old beliefs and knowledge in handling disasters. From the earlier research, many a time local wisdom has proven useful especially in disaster preparedness. In some counties a strong wind blowing from the eastern side and the unexplained sound of thunder from the direction of the sea means the likelihood of a cyclone. For predicting floods, communities in the flood-prone areas make an assumption of the likelihood of future flood by looking at the color of clouds, and most importantly, to the cloud formation. For example, in Nepal, during the monsoon period, people may observe the level of water in the river, as they apply traditional beliefs and intuitive power in perception to see any strange changes in regard to the formation and the level of water. The intuitive power of observation helps communities to gain preparation time as to when to evacuate their homes for safety, and collecting necessary items (Medury 2008).

It is noteworthy that individual decision-making before disaster is different due to varying prior experience and culture, gender, and the reliability of warning signals (Cutter and Gall 2006). However, there have been differentiated impact of disasters on men and women primarily in developing countries, since women are a disadvantaged group regarding access to job, and access to decision-making. Thus women are largely excluded in society and have minimal control over resources. Note also that physical and psychological vulnerabilities of women are present in society. It is important to note that a gender-friendly approach was lacking in disaster management policy, but it is now gradually being adopted in the policy framework in many countries in their disaster and emergency planning for preparedness, response, and recovery. The growing role of women is undeniable, as they can help male members in disasters. Women in general, discharge multifaceted roles and functions in disaster situations, in providing primary health care to their own family members, and attempt to fulfill the needs of three necessary commodities in life such as food, water, and fuel (Medury 2008).

Flooding is a common natural disaster in some parts of Bangladesh. During the flood, the role of women is evident in safe food handling, storage, and preparation for their family members. For example, it is observed that in Faridpur district, women securely store puffed rice and dried coconuts in suitable locations in case of food shortages. Quite interestingly, this kind of food has long durability and fulfills the requirement of sufficient energy during the disaster. Women in the flood-prone areas also make sure that daily necessary items including some clothes and sets of sleeping beds are kept very carefully so that the other family members can use them for several days when the level of floodwater further rises (Medury 2008).

After the devastating tsunami, many women's organizations at the local level in India have initiated programs and activities toward strengthening resilience at the community level. These women were the survivors of the tsunami. Along with the government, and the NGOs, the women's groups voluntarily trained other disaster-affected families in society on how to enhance adaptive power and recovery processes. An NGO, Sanghamithra Service Society, working in the coastal region of Andhra Pradesh formed a community disaster preparedness team. Initially, due to cultural dogma the men had been hesitant to let women join these teams, but a moral argument came from the women's group that preparedness plan was important for the safety of their own families and communities during disasters. Once a group of "disaster preparedness team of women" is formed, they themselves had been involved in organizing disaster preparedness and response training to other people in different areas (Medury 2008).

There is another justification of community-based approach for post-disaster reconstruction. Johnson and Olshansky (2016) found that after the devastating 2004 Indian Ocean tsunami, it forced Indonesia to introduce a community-driven approach for reconstruction purposes, which is called Community-Based Settlement Rehabilitation and Reconstruction Project. At the beginning, due to the largescale of its impact on the country, some opposed the idea of community-based approach. Although it was adopted as an experimental project, it became a highly successful strategy for reconstruction in Indonesian disasters over the past decade (Johnson and Olshansky 2016).

Coordination and Collaboration in Disaster Management

Immediately after a disaster, the most persistent challenge in disaster response is that no one is in charge of dealing with it. For example, in the immediate aftermath of the Gujarat earthquake in 2001, there was a desperate need for coordination and collaboration to ensure speedy relief distribution among the affected people. Upon the request of the government of Gujarat, large-scale relief commodities and supplies reached the point for distribution, but it was observed that there were lapses in the coordination between government institutions and national and international NGOs (Moore et al. 2007). Hence, strong and inclusive coordination and collaboration in disaster management among different stakeholders at the local level should become an important agenda in the disaster management framework and convention.

On the other hand, technological advancement in early warning systems facilitate and support agencies involved incoordination in the disaster preparedness process for the State of Hawaii (Prizzia 2008). For effective disaster preparedness, it requires a proper understanding and knowledge of various categories of disasters, and its policy of how to connect involved agencies as regards coordination and collaboration. It is already argued that there is a need for continuous training in disaster management that supports coordination and collaboration at the local levels (Prizzia 2008). More to an empirical case, a major challenge emerged after Nepal's earthquake of 2015 that effective disaster management efforts require proper data collection, and its effective utilization for sound planning, monitoring, evaluation, and feedback. It is quite interesting to note that Habitat for Humanity Nepal (HFHN) have recently initiated mobile and web GIS system to the disaster-prone areas for helping out to the affected communities during the recovery and rehabilitation stages.

Technologically developed early warning systems and remote sensing have contributed significantly to the course of disaster management in reducing casualties and destruction of properties and also helped with the appropriate decision-making of the disaster management authorities. In an empirical study conducted by the Commission of the African Union in 2008, it has been reported that sub-Saharan Africa has the highest mortality rate due to droughts compared to any other regions in the world (van Aalst et al. 2013). Van Aalst et al. (2013) also point out that the 2011 famine crisis in Africa exemplifies how existing early warning systems failed to avert famine. Millions in sub-Saharan African countries, mostly in Somalia, suffered from hunger, and hundreds of thousands died.

However, classical organizational theorists have always argued for a supportive structure and functions in order to bring solutions of many of the coordination complexities. Famous organization theorist Luther Gulick explains,

> Wherever many men are thus working together the best results are secured when there is a division of work among these men. The theory of organization, therefore, has to do with the structure of coordination imposed upon the work-division units of an enterprise. (Gulick 1937, cited by Prizzia 2008, p. 81)

The above observation was seen in the case of Hurricane Katrina, which still remains the deadliest natural disaster in the history of the United Sates. Data shows that Hurricane Katrina caused almost 1,200 deaths in states including Louisiana, Mississippi, and Alabama. Apart from that the storm caused hundreds of thousands of people to be reported homeless or displaced, and tens of billions of dollars of worth in economic losses. This unprecedented failure of response to disasters forced the government and various organizations to form several inquiries committees, and a session on special hearing was organized by the U.S. Senate Homeland Security and Governmental Affairs Committee. One of the most important find-ings was explained as "*Political Appointments, Bureau Chiefs and Federal Management Performance,*" it says that before and after the storm govern-ment executives performed better in handling emergency management than the politically appointed heads of agencies (Prizzia 2008).

A success story is the case of Sichuan Province in China. In 2008 after a magnitude 7.9 earthquake caused the death of 69,226 people. As an immediate response, China's Premier Wen Jiabao, introduced the *Post-Earthquake Reconstruction Planning Group* (Johnson and Olshansky 2016). The mission of the formed group was to maintain a quick recovery for the affected people and their livelihood. Within2years of the incident, all housing repair was successfully completed. Two million new units of rural housing, 290,000 units of new urban housing were constructed (Johnson and Olshansky 2016). This success was only possible because the central government made recovery apriority on the national agenda, and officials were held accountable for their actions in regard to reconstruction plans.

Apart from contributing relief and assistance to disasters, the inter-national community can do very little for saving lives, if they are not fam-iliar with the affected local areas, or are notable to comprehend the actual needs of the affected people or the uninformed local culture. However, financial support from the international community is definitely important for reconstruction, medical assistance for primary aid, and in the recovery stages necessary commodities such as food and water. But it is important to make a note that the assistance received from the international commun-ity has to be coordinated with local offices and their efforts. The approach of working collaboratively has to be coordinated and maintained with the hierarchy of authorities; otherwise, disaster management efforts may suffer. Another example of complexity of coordination problem has been found in the case of the December 2004 tsunami. There was, however, a great deal of anomalies during the relief and rehabilitation phase due to the lack of coordination after the Indian Ocean Tsunami of 2004 (Pinkowski 2008b).

Local Demographic Characteristics

According to the United Nations (UN), a large number of the popula-tion live below the poverty line (US$1/person/day) (Murray et al. 2012).

Poverty increases the risks of proneness to disasters. It is proven that poverty increases vulnerabilities in coping with a natural disaster in diverse ways. For example, poverty-stricken people must live in poor housing conditions with inadequate resources to effectively respond to a disaster. The poor do not have adequate resources for the construction of quality housing, therefore they are more likely to experience destruction of their homes. In many instances in the coastal areas, poor people are not able to protect their home, which increases the likelihood of loss of life, injury, or destruction.

It is also plain to see that vulnerability usually occurs when there is tremendous pressure to accommodate an increased population, and land is unduly sacrificed for their accommodation. It is observed that "*flood plains and unstable hillsides become sites for housing, often informal and low-quality housing, because there is no other land available at reasonable cost, sufficiently close to employment opportunities*" (Misomali and McEntire 2008, p. 28). For example, on June11, 2007 heavy rainfall during the monsoon period caused huge mudslides in the second largest city in Bangladesh, Chittagong, which killed 128 people (Rubel and Ahmed 2013) and injured thousands. However, environmental experts blamed the government of Bangladesh for its failure in taking any stern action against those who cut into the hill illegally.

Furthermore, a special feature of demographics, such as growing population and rapid urbanization, is that it increases vulnerabilities of these groups to disasters. More to the point, when people reside in densely populated areas, there is a higher possibility of catastrophic consequences from natural or man-made disasters. It is plain to see in the event of September 11, 2001 wherealmost3,000 people were killed after a hijacked airplane (Bell 2018) struck the South and North Twin Towers in New York City.

Strong Disaster Management Agencies

Australia has developed disaster risk management by employing different strategies that include campaigning for disaster risks awareness, improving warning systems and its awareness, disaster information sharing between government and the citizens, developing integrated long-term disaster plans, and sufficient budgetary allocation for disaster risk management (Murray et al. 2012). It is worth mentioning that a weak emergency management institution at the local level hampers the disaster management process. For example, Hurricane Katrina in the United States provides glaring empirical evidence of how a weak local government institution might be ineffective in handling emergency preparedness plans. For instance, the city of New Orleans government had evacuation routes and maps for the affected people, but it became clear immediately after the storm that the plan did not work well (Misomali and McEntire 2008). Both the print and electronic media supplied images of affected people waiting in their own buildings to be evacuated, although there were a lot of buses parked in the school. People expressed dissatisfaction over the services of the buses, because these buses did not arrive before the storm, thus, they were not able to avail the opportunity of evacuation plan. It is plain to see that local officials failed to synchronize the evacuation plan, and also failed to provide early messages to the affected people on when and how they could take bus services and support (Misomali and McEntire 2008). This situation indicates the failure of New Orleans government for a safe evacuation before the storm. In essence, a country may have a good written strategic preparedness plan, but it will not bring about any success stories in emergency operations, because it does not have much time and effort put into it in advance to ensure the emergency evacuation plan works.

Conclusion and Lessons Learned

The worst consequences of a natural disaster occurs in a social context where vulnerabilities and lack of resources challenge disaster preparedness and disaster mitigation. Hence, it is very important to properly understand the complexity of actors and factors involved in planning and implementing disaster management. It requires an organized efforts and sharing information and knowledge at different levels on disaster management strategies that will help for the future disaster management practices. In conclusion, strategies for preventing loss of life, injuries, and destruction of property resulting from the natural disasters requires participation of the local community at all levels. This will create a disaster-resilient society, but they must fully understand the disaster preparedness plan, and apply it in their own disaster-prone areas. Community and other stakeholders involved in emergency management should mobilize their efforts and spend time at the local affected areas in order to help any response efforts in the process of disaster management. However, keeping the lessons of the past disasters in mind, all countries in the world should develop better response and recovery strategies for future plan of actions.

References

Bell, C. 2018. "The People Who Think 9/11 may Have Been an 'Inside Job'." *British Broadcasting Corporation (BBC) Trending*, 1 February, 2018. https://www.bbc.com/news/blogs-trending-42195513

Cagliuso, N. V., Sr, E. J. Lazar, A. N. Lazar, and L. J. Berger. 2008. "Hospital Emergency Preparedness." In *Disaster Management Handbook*, ed. J. Pinkowski, Chapter 18, pp. 370–83. Boca Raton, FL: CRC Press, Taylor & Francis Group. Public Administration and Public Policy/138 (A Comprehensive Publication Program).

Chan, M.2015. "U.N. Study: Natural Disasters Caused 600,000 Deaths Over 20 Years." *Time Newsletters*, November 23, 2015. http://time.com/4124755/natural-disasters-death-united-nations

CRED (Center for Research on the Epidemiology of Disasters). 2007. "Annual Disaster Statistical Review: The Numbers and Trends." [Online] http://www.preventionweb.net/files/1080_Annual20Disaster20 Statistical20Review202006.pdf

CRED (Centre for Research on the Epidemiology of Disasters). 2016. "Poverty & Death: Disaster and Mortality 1996-2015." *UN office for Disaster Risk Reduction*, 12 October 2016. https://reliefweb.int/report/world/poverty-death-disaster-and-mortality-1996-2015

Cutter, S. L., and M. Gall. 2006. "Hurricane Katrina: A Failure of Planning or a Planned Failure?" In *Naturrisiken und Sozialkatastrophen*, eds. C. Felgentreff and T. Glade, Chapter 27, pp. 1–20. Columbia, SC: Hazards Research Lab, Department of Geography, University of South Carolina.

Hendriks, E., Ir., M. Basso, D. Sposini, L. Ewijk, and H. Jurkowska. n.d. *Self-built Housing as an Alternative for Post-disaster Recovery.* Eindhoven University of Technology, the Netherlands. https://www.ethz. ch/content/dam/ethz/special-interest/conference-websites-dam/no-cost-housing-dam/documents/Hendriks_Paper.pdf

IPCC (Intergovernmental Panel on Climate Change). 2000. "Presentation of Robert Watson, Chair, Intergovernmental Panel on Climate Change, at the Sixth Conference of the Parties to the United Nations Framework Convention on Climate Change." *The Hague,* November 13, 2000.

Jenkins, S. 2015. "Resilience: The New Paradigm in Disaster Management—An Australian Perspective." *World Journal of Engineering and Technology* 3, no. 3, pp. 129–39.

Johnson, L.A., and R. B. Olshansky. 2016. *After Great Disasters: How Six Countries Managed Community Recovery.* Cambridge, MA: Policy Focus Report, Lincoln Institute of Land Policy, pp. 1–76.

Medury, U.2008. "Toward Disaster Resilient Communities: A New Approach for South Asia and Africa." In *Disaster Management Handbook,* ed. J. Pinkowski, Chapter 16, (pp. 338–53). Boca Raton, FL: CRC Press, Taylor & Francis Group. Public Administration and Public Policy/138 (A Comprehensive Publication Program).

Misomali, R., and D. McEntire.2008. "Rising Disasters and Their Reversal: An Identification of Vulnerability and Ways to Reduce It." In *Disaster Management Handbook,* ed. J. Pinkowski, Chapter 2, pp. 20–34. Boca Raton, FL: CRC Press, Taylor & Francis Group. Public Administration and Public Policy/138 (A Comprehensive Publication Program).

Moeller, B.J. 2008. "National Incident Management System: Bringing Order to Chaos." In *Disaster Management Handbook,* ed. J. Pinkowski, Chapter 17, pp. 358–67. Boca Raton, FL: CRC Press, Taylor & Francis Group. Public Administration and Public Policy/138 (A Comprehensive Publication Program).

Moore, M., H. R. Trujillo, B. K. Stearns, R. Basurtodavila, and D. Evans. 2007. "Models of Relief Learning from Exemplary Practices in International Disaster Management." *Prepared for RAND Center for Domestic and International Health Security* WR-514, pp. 1–262.

Murray, V., G. McBean, M. Bhatt, S. Borsch, T. S. Cheong, W. F. Erian, S. Llosa, et al. 2012. "Case studies. In: Managing the Risks of Extreme Events and Disasters to Advance Climate Change Adaptation." In *A Special Report of Working Groups I and II of the Intergovernmental Panel on Climate Change (IPCC)*, eds. C. B. Field, V. Barros, T.F. Stocker, D. Qin, D. J. Dokken, K. L. Ebi, M. D. Mastrandrea, et al., pp. 487–542. Cambridge, UK: Cambridge University Press.

Pinkowski, J. 2008a. *Disaster Management Handbook*. Boca Raton, FL: CRC Press, Taylor & Francis Group. Public Administration and Public Policy/138 (A Comprehensive Publication Program).

Pinkowski, J. 2008b. "Coastal Development and Disaster Preparedness: The Delusion of Preparedness in Face of Overwhelming Forces." In *Disaster Management Handbook,* ed. J. Pinkowski, pp. 4–15. Boca Raton, FL: CRC Press, Taylor & Francis Group. Public Administration and Public Policy/138 (A Comprehensive Publication Program).

Powers, R.2008. "Issues in Hospital Preparedness." In *Disaster Management Handbook*, ed. J. Pinkowski, Chapter 30, pp. 562–69. Boca Raton, FL: CRC Press, Taylor & Francis Group. Public Administration and Public Policy/138 (A Comprehensive Publication Program).

Prizzia, R. 2008. "The Role of Coordination in Disaster Management." In *Disaster Management Handbook*, ed. J. Pinkowski, Chapter 5, pp. 76–96. Boca Raton, FL: CRC Press, Taylor & Francis Group. Public Administration and Public Policy/138 (A Comprehensive Publication Program).

Quyyum, M.A. 2015. "Managing Disasters Scientifically." *The Daily Star* (An English Daily Newspaper), March 31, 2015. https://www.thedailystar .net/op-ed/managing-disasters-scientifically-74645

Rubel, Y. A., and B. Ahmed. 2013. "Understanding the Issues Involved in Urban Landslide Vulnerability in Chittagong Metropolitan Area, Bangladesh."http://discovery.ucl.ac.uk/1418959/1/Final%20Report_ Yiaser_Bayes _Bangladesh.pdf

Sonny, J. 1999. "Fundamentals of Disaster Risk Management: How are Southeast Asian Countries Addressing this?" In *Risk, Development and Disasters: Southern Perspectives,* University of Cape Town, Department of Environment and Geographical Sciences.

Van Aalst, M., J. Kellett, F. Pichon, and T. Mitchell. 2013. "Incentives in Disaster Risk Management and Humanitarian Response." *Background Note for World Development Report 2014*, Red Cross Climate Center and Overseas Development Institute, pp. 1–20.

Withanaarachchi, J., and S. Setunge. 2014. "Influence of Decision Making During Disasters and How It Impacts a Community." In *10th International Conference of the International Institute for Infrastructure Resilience and Reconstruction (I3R2)*, 20–22 May, 2014, pp. 176–88. West Lafayette, IN: Purdue University.

CHAPTER 3

The Paradigm Shift in Disaster Management in Bangladesh

Mahfuzul Haque
Independent Researcher
Dhaka, Bangladesh

Introduction

Bangladesh is one of the most disaster-prone countries in the world. Floods, tropical cyclones, tornadoes, tidal surges, droughts, and river bank erosion continue to disrupt lives and livelihoods of the poor people in disaster-prone areas, especially in the southwestern coastal region of Bangladesh. The very geographical location of Bangladesh over the conical shape of Bay of Bengal attracts periodic cyclones and associated tidal surges. The country's vulnerability to natural disaster is rooted in its geographic location in the world's largest delta associated with a series of hydro-meteorological and geophysical factors (GOB 2009a). Out of 35 million people in 710 km stretch of coastal areas of Bangladesh, 7 million people live in a high disaster risk zone. Although, there was damages of properties and crops during the cyclones of *Sidr* in 2007 and *Aila* in 2009, the loss of human lives was only 3,406 and 190, respectively (Ministry of Disaster Management and Relief Bangladesh Secretariat 2012), which might help to draw a conclusion that perhaps effective networking and coordination between and among various levels of the government and nongovernment organizations (NGOs) concerning disaster risk reduction and preparedness programs did help to a great extent. During the earlier days, loss of lives and property was very severe during disasters like floods and cyclones. Cyclones of 1970 and 1991 killed as many as 330,000 and 138,882 people, respectively, in the coast of Bangladesh (GOB 2009a, p. 2). Massive awareness of the local community in recent days supported by updated cyclone warning systems, campaign of cyclone volunteers and developed electronic media played an important role in managing cyclones and related tidal surges these days.

Disaster management practices have developed over a period of time from a traditional top-down relief and response to a more integrated risk management method (Yodmani 2001). In recent years, there has been a paradigm shift in disaster management from post-disaster relief operation and rehabilitation to disaster risk reduction (The United Nations [UN], 2014). Disaster Management includes all aspects of planning and response to disasters. Both the risk and the consequences of disasters are addressed through disaster management. It suggests that prevention and preparedness measures are taken well in advance prior to the hazards ("pre-disaster" situation). There is a long-term rehabilitation (often referred to as "post-disaster reconstruction") program in order to prepare the local community for facing the wrath of disaster with confidence (Task Force for Disaster, Community Readiness, and Recovery, The Society for Community Research and Action 2010).

In earlier times, disasters were considered as a sudden onslaught and responded by the governments, donor agencies, relief and rehabilitation organizations and they often do not address the causes of disasters. As a result, there were recurrence of disasters, which continued to cause deaths and damages without respite. Traditional policy planners used to put an emphasis mostly on disaster relief operation, which later gradually changed to an emphasis on disaster risk reduction and various long-term preparedness programs concerning disasters (National Plan for Disaster Management [NPDM] 2010 to 2015). This contingency planning did improve efficiency of the Cyclone Preparedness Program (CPP) volunteers and other relief agencies.

Over the four decades from the 1960s to the 1990s, there has been an increase in disaster-led human casualties and material losses across the globe. Yodmani stated that disaster-led damages and deaths varies from region to region depending on its socioeconomic development (Yodmani

2001, p. 2). A classic example given by Frederick Cuny (1983), stated that an earthquake of 6.4 magnitude (Richter scale) in California in 1971 caused only 58 deaths, while another earthquake in 1973 of lesser magnitude of 6.2 destroyed the central city of Managua, Nicaragua, causing the death of 6,000 people. It shows how a disaster can impact a locality depends primarily on the vulnerability of the community. Emphasis was given on "vulnerability analysis" as a tool in disaster management. This has led to a more comprehensive approach to disaster risk management. This approach has put emphasis on enhancement of management capacity following vulnerability analysis and hazard assessment. Disasters then are seen as not necessarily caused by nature but as consequences of faulty development activities. It is now recognized that unmanaged or mismanaged risks for a longer period of time would cause disasters.

Paradigm shift from relief and response to risk management has started to influence and guide policy makers and planners engaged in disaster management. Following this paradigm shift, in some countries, plans and programs were taken to reduce social and economic vulnerability and the undertaking of long-term mitigation and adaptation measures. There is a long way to go as these initiatives are yet to receive the priority of the development partners. Moreover, the poor are always left behind. The challenge is how to mainstream this paradigm shift in development plans and policies as emphasis is given on good governance, accountability, and bottom-up participatory methods. Similarly, community-based disaster management (CBDM), a term coined by the development practitioners, also gaining ground as increasing emphasis is given on the merit of traditional knowledge and practices in disaster management.

The chapter is mainly based on the secondary sources of literature. Available books and articles published in peer-reviewed journals were consulted. The overall goal of this chapter is to look at this paradigm shift in disaster management from traditional relief and rehabilitation to disaster risk reduction and to see whether there has been less deaths and loss of properties in the coastal districts of Bangladesh due to this paradigm shift. The chapter argues that the paradigm shifts from responding after a disaster to pre-disaster mitigation and preparedness through coordination and networking among various tiers of the local and the central government is a necessary and cost-effective approach in disaster management.

The chapter has been structured as follows: the first section has given a general introduction on the vulnerability of Bangladesh due to her geophysical conditions; traditional relief and rehabilitation approaches of the past; and loss of lives due to devastating cyclones. The second section deals with the global scenario including that of Hyogo Framework (2005 to 2015); Sendai Framework (2015 to 2030), and Paris Climate Agreement 2015. The third section highlights the plans, policies, and guidelines including that of the Standing Orders on Disaster (SOD) 2010 adopted by the Government of Bangladesh targeting disaster risk reduction (DRR) issues. The fourth section summarizes the best practices being followed by Bangladesh in DRR. The fifth section deals with the CBDM in practice. The next section focuses on the future challenges to be faced in implementing this paradigm shift; and the last section contains conclusions and suggestions.

Global Scenario

Due to global warming and emissions of greenhouse gases, natural disasters are on the rise both in frequency and ferocity affecting the livelihood of the rural poor. Disaster risk has increasingly become a global concern. Against the backdrop of this alarming situation, some of the unfolding global events to manage it are as follows.

Hyogo Framework (2005 to 2015)

World Conference on Disaster Reduction, held in 2005, adopted the Hyogo Framework for Action (HFA) 2005 to 2015. The Agreement urged upon the participants to follow an integrated multihazard approach for sustainable development in order to reduce both the intensity and frequency of disasters. The Conference promoted a strategic and systematic approach to reduce vulnerabilities and risks to hazards. It underscored the need for building the resilience of people in risk-prone areas. (Hyogo 2015).

Sendai Framework (2015 to 2030)

Hyogo Framework for Action was followed by adoption of Sendai Framework for Disaster Risk Reduction in March 2015 (UN, 2015). The

Sendai Framework sent a strong message to the world community that reducing risk to disasters was the effective way in managing a disaster. It called for reduction of disaster risk by preventing new and existing risk and strengthening community resilience. The Framework provided a set of guiding principles, which clarified that it was the prime responsibility of a state to help prevent a disaster including that of disaster preparedness. Moreover, the range of disaster risk reduction widened to include both natural and man-made hazards including environmental, technological and biological hazards.

The international community also recognized contribution of indigenous knowledge and practices on disaster risk reduction, climate change, and natural resource management. The Sendai Framework put an emphasis on indigenous knowledge and practices and coping strategies of the local community in facing challenges of a natural disaster. Highlighting the role of the stakeholders, it stressed the contribution of the indigenous peoples through their experience and traditional knowledge in implementation of various international guidelines. The Framework stated that the indigenous knowledge and practices would support scientific knowledge in disaster risk assessment and help mainstream in national plans and policies.

Paris UN Climate Conference 2015

Twenty-first Conference of the Parties (COP-21) to UN Framework Convention on Climate Change (UNFCCC) held in Paris, France in December 2015, adopted the "Paris Agreement," which put an emphasis on the involvement of local communities in disaster risk reduction. Countries agreed to limit global warming well below 2°C compared to preindustrial levels. It is generally understood that by undertaking mitigation measures through reducing greenhouse gas emissions, disaster risk is reduced by a great extent. There is no doubt that if we achieve reduction of greenhouse gases to a warming of 1.5°C, it would immensely contribute to reduction in disaster losses. The Paris Agreement, to be made effective from 2020, signed and ratified by 55 countries accounting for 55 percent of global emissions. The United States and China account for 40 percent of global emissions and, alarmingly, US president Donald Trump announced withdrawal from the Paris Agreement.

Meanwhile, the 23rd Conference of Parties (COP-23), which took place in Bonn, Germany in 2017, focused primarily on challenges of the implementation of the agreement as the agreement is expected to come into force in 2020. It was the first conference of parties to take place after President Trump decided to pull out of the agreement.

Bangladesh Scenario

During the start of the new century, a series of plans, policies, and action plans were adopted by the government targeting reducing disaster impacts. In line with the Hyogo Framework, Bangladesh adopted the SOD in 2010, which described the role and responsibilities of various tiers of the government from central to local level involved in disaster risk reduction and emergency response. SOD detailed out risk reduction activities to be undertaken by various agencies during the warning period and during the disaster and postdisaster periods (GOB 2010a). It has become a unique document for the volunteers and officials engaged in disaster management.

Another important document, the NPDM 2010 to 2015 of Bangladesh followed a model aiming at disaster risk reduction and emergency response. The model has three key components, "which are defining the risk environment; managing the risk environment; and responding to the threat environment" (GOB 2010a, p. 2; GOB 2010b, p. 37). The Plan promoted understanding of the social, political, and community environment; establishing likely threats; examining likely consequences; ranking risks; and identifying actions to eliminate, reduce, or manage risk. The second element promoted community-based adaptation programs; and the third element helped the disaster management officials to understand the difference between risk reduction and emergency response (GOB 2010a, p. 2; GOB 2010b, p. 38). Response included "warning period (alert and activation); disaster onset (response); and post-disaster period (relief, early recovery and rehabilitation)" (GOB 2010a, p. 3). The government adopted the Bangladesh National Disaster Management Guidelines in 2015, which in its objectives put more emphasis on disaster risk reduction and food and livelihood security. The Guidelines laid out an emphasis on adaptation to climate change and overall disaster risk reduction (GOB 2015, p. 7251). It is noteworthy that the draft National Plan for Disaster Management (2016 to 2020) with caption, "Building Resilience for Sustainable Human Development" in its mission statement stated that the Plan would achieve

> a paradigm shifts in disaster management from conventional response and relief to more comprehensive risk reduction culture, and to promote food security as an important factor in ensuring the resilience of communities to hazards. (GOB 2017, p.1)

The new plan would be a live and adaptive document in line with changes taking place in relation to disaster management.

Plans and policies cannot be enforced unless followed by legislations. Accordingly, the Disaster Management Act 2012 was enacted, which made provision of setting up of an authority to try offenders responsible for the failure to reduce disaster risks; failure in protecting lives and livelihoods of people; failure to predict and undertake contingency measures relating to natural disasters, etc. (GOB 2012, sections 36 to 51). The Act suggested a national fund for disaster response, relief, and rehabilitation activities, and it could declare an area as a "Distressed Area" in order to prevent people from undertaking any destructive activities. Earlier, embankments were damaged, holes were made allowing intrusion of saline water for shrimp cultivation which caused serious damages to embankments during storm surges. It would create water logging and there was no punishment for the offenders. Under this act, offenders could be tried—a major breakthrough in disaster management.

Best Practices in Disaster Risk Reduction

Bangladesh is one of the first few countries to have integrated disaster management into poverty reduction strategies and in macro-level plans like the five-year plans and long-term visionary plans. NPDM 2010 to 2015 has completed its term and draft NPDM 2016 to 2020 (GOB 2017, p. 1) is a follow-up of the earlier plan. It differs in framework because of alignment with recent global agreements including Sendai Framework on DRR, Climate Change Agreement, and the SDGs. Some of the best practices (GOB 2009a, p. 1) in DRR being followed by Bangladesh could be summarized as follows.

A) **Paradigm shift—from relief and rehabilitation to risk reduction:** The biggest challenge that Bangladesh has embraced is changing the way disaster management is understood and practiced at national and community levels. Necessary DRR policies, institutions, and processes have been undertaken including comprehensive disaster management program and SOD.

B) **Effective early warning at the community level:** CPP with early warning dissemination with adequate lead time for saving many lives and property. In flood areas, communities have devised mechanisms to disseminate a flood warning system.

C) **Community empowerment and resilience:** CBDM is based on indigenous knowledge and practices and resilience. People are being empowered through community risk assessment, participatory risk reduction action plan, etc.

D) **Reducing risk factors:** Building cyclone shelters, flood shelters, *killa*, disaster-proof low-cost rural housing greatly reduce disaster risks. In case of agriculture, crop varieties tolerant to salinity, flooding, and drought are introduced. Afforestation done in the coastal belts to combat onslaught of cyclonic storms.

E) **Reducing loss of lives:** Response to supercyclone like *Sidr* of 2007; *Aila* of 2009, and floods of 1998 and 2007 could be an example of lesser loss of lives and damages to properties due to effective disaster management.

The country could boast of some of these best practices in disaster risk reduction. Focus on climate change–induced disasters has been in national plans and policies. Implementation of some of these plans (National Adaptation Programme of Actions (NAPA) 2009, Bangladesh Climate Change Strategy and Action Plan (BCCSAP) 2009) aptly reflect the country's readiness in effective disaster risk reduction (MoEF 2009a, 2009b). Since climate change–induced disasters are development concerns, both NAPA and BCCSAP put emphasis on creating a synergy between disaster risk reduction and climate change adaptation (Islam and Sumon 2013, p. 84).

A comparative analysis of four major cyclones in the last 40 years and their aftermaths in the coast of Bangladesh has been done. Due to lack of proper strategy and directions 330,000 people died in the Great Bhola cyclone of 1970 and another 138,882 people died in Gorky in 1991. Following the paradigm shift in disaster management and implementation of good practices, only 3,406 people died in cyclone *Sidr* in 2007 and another 190 in *Aila* in 2009 (GOB 2009a;). The comparatively low number of deaths caused by cyclones *Sidr* and *Aila* suggests that the paradigm shift in disaster management might have played a role. Recent calamities saw timely cyclone forecasting and early warnings, and successful evacuation of coastal communities. Moreover, under the CPP initiated after 1970 cyclone, nearly 43,000 CPP volunteers (out of which, 14,225 are women) are responsible for disseminating cyclone warnings among villagers via megaphones and by house-to-house contact (GOB 2009a, p. 6). CPP volunteers visit the affected communities and spread cyclone warning and evacuation orders via megaphones and bicycle-mounted loudspeakers.

Among other measures, the Storm Warning Center (SWC), Metrological forecasting and warnings have been made user-friendly. Currently, there are around 4,000 cyclone shelters providing security to coastal people. These cyclone shelters were constructed back in 1972 to protect coastal residents from cyclones and storm surges. These are multistoried buildings, built above the ground-level in order to resist storm surges, and they can accommodate 500 to 2,500 people. It could be said that strict adherence to SOD 2010 and National Plan for Disaster Management (NPDM) 2010 to 2015 were a factor in the reduction of casualties and less damage to properties.

Community-based Disaster Management

Due to global warming, climate change–induced disasters like cyclones and tidal surges periodically hit the coast of Bangladesh and the country is one of the most vulnerable countries of the world. Over the years, the coastal community has developed some indigenous practices to combat disasters. Community-based adaptation to climate change is a community-led practice, based on the priorities set by the communities themselves in line with their priorities and needs. It seeks to empower people to prepare for and cope with the impacts of climate change (Reid and Schipper 2014, p. 7).

According to Pandey (2005), CBDM promotes participatory planning based on grassroots-based consultation. Community-based disaster risk reduction aims to reduce the vulnerability and enhance the resilience of local communities to the impacts of disaster (Gero, Meheux, and Dominey-Howes 2011, p. 102). CBDM helps the local community to understand their vulnerabilities to hazard and develop their capacities to face a disaster. They are aware of the fact that they are the first ones to be hit by a disaster. They evaluate their own strength and weakness in the face of an impending disaster and undertake strategies accordingly. Through this process, the local community not only becomes a part of the plans and decisions, but also becomes an actor in their implementation.

How do they survive during and after a cyclonic disaster? What are the indigenous survival strategies? Women and children are the most vulnerable groups as they are confined in homes and less mobile than men (GOB 2009b, p. 18). In a study conducted on the people of the coastal islands, it was revealed that the islanders have developed certain short-term survival strategies of their own (Hassan 2000, p. 149). Survival strategies include holding onto and binding themselves to trees; looking for comparatively safer places like embankments and polders; using floating logs, thatched roof, straw piles, and bunches of coconuts.

People of the locality have also devised appropriate methods for food preservation during cyclones and tidal surges. Self-protection instinct dominated the indigenous survival strategy. The women prefer putting on *Salwar* and *Kamiz* dress instead of *Saris* (traditional female dress in South Asia), as the later makes it difficult to swim (Haque 2013, p. 282). In the aftermath of a disaster, coping strategies work well with the help of the community members to their mutual benefit. Generally, outside help and relief goods appear 2 to 3 days after the disaster. What do they do during this intervening period? People eat stems and roots of edible plants. For drinking purposes, they drink rain water, as cyclones are always followed by rain for several hours. In the absence of rainwater, they share coconut water. According to Nasreen (2000, p. 77), women in flood-hit areas, use herbal medicine for the prevention of diarrhea or dysentery. They use the juice of certain leaves to stop bleeding of injuries.

Among structural measures, the people in the coast are seen using roofing materials and design (sloping the wind direction). They plant local varieties of plants surrounding their homesteads. They raise the plinth level of their houses, construct *killas* (raised earth) for shelter of their cattle during a disaster. Another interesting phenomenon was that during tidal surges, people tied rafts to coconut trees so that they rose and fell with the level of the water (Haque 2000, p. 142; Haque 2017, p. 181).

Future Challenges

Aiming at achieving disaster risk reduction, Bangladesh faces a number of challenges in effecting the paradigm shift, which are as follows:

A) The mindset of the people, the victims, is to be changed. The primitive notion that the donors would come with relief materials is no more there in disaster parlance these days. Under the disaster risk reduction, people are prepared for the predisaster and postdisaster period.

B) There is another notion, that distribution of relief materials among the victims is the sole responsibility of the government and the voluntary agencies during the period of disaster, which needs to be changed as well. According to SOD, various committees at village and upazilla levels are entrusted with the responsibilities to prepare people to face a disaster. Trained volunteers are there to rescue people from the disaster.

C) Sometimes it is found that the associated administrators are not willing to accept the views of the rural poor community during the policy formulation process—a mindset that needs to be changed.

D) In the absence of a common forum or lack of interagency coordination or confusion of jurisdiction of work, lack of mutual trust and respect often poses threats for CBDM.

E) Women and children mostly remain at home and are less mobile than men. It is often found that women do not want to leave their residence and take shelter in the cyclone shelters mainly due to lack of privacy, security, and sanitation facilities. They are often found to be vulnerable to sexual harassment during pre- and postdisaster situations.

F) Persons with disabilities are one of the most vulnerable groups and suffer the most during disasters. They are often neglected and left alone to face the wrath of a disaster. Trained volunteers could rescue them.

G) Indigenous communities, particularly those living in remote areas with different language and culture, face injury and loss from the effects of natural disasters. They are to be included and consulted in the community risk assessment guidelines.

H) Regular training of national and local volunteers is required, and allocation of adequate financial resources is necessary. Effective coordination between and among various agencies of the government at all levels and the nongovernment agencies continue to remain a challenge.

I) Continued good governance is a prerequisite to an effective disaster risk reduction program. Continuation of such a disaster management governance is a big challenge, which needs to be overcome.

Conclusion

It is evident that disasters like cyclones, tornadoes, and tidal surges will continue to visit the coast of Bangladesh and they cannot be controlled. Only through better management practices, damages can be reduced to a large extent. Bangladesh over the years was able to decrease the number of deaths and loss of properties, mainly due to this paradigm shift reflected in various plans, policies, guidelines, and action plans adopted by the government from time to time. Bangladesh's disaster management model did attract attention of the global community, as they have been striving to reduce casualties due to increasing disasters. The challenge remains to be the effective implementation and updating of the standing orders of, and rigorous monitoring by, the authorities for their enforcement. Dilapidated cyclone shelters need urgent renovation. Periodic training of the CPP volunteers is essential for a fruitful implementation of the new strategy shift.

CBDM is in a nascent stage and needs promotion and nurturing. Promotion of CBDM is a painstaking process, requiring continuous research and development in consultation with the vulnerable communities. Such a program has to be people-centered, process-oriented, community-led, knowledge-oriented, empowerment-focused, and accountability-driven. Time and again, people of disaster-prone areas have proved that instead of structural methods, local indigenous knowledge and practices have solved many problems related to a natural disaster.

The support of the government and the development partners is necessary to develop successful models concerning CBDM. Various initiatives undertaken by local and international NGOs and research bodies are to continue in order to mainstream it into all plans and policies at the national and global levels. There are many challenges. To overcome these challenges, good environmental governance is necessary, which would be transparent and pro-people, and practice democratic norms. The Parliamentary Committee on Disaster Management needs to be made effective. To achieve these goals, continuity of good environmental governance is a prerequisite.

References

Cuny, F. 1983. *Disasters and Development.* ed. Susan Abrams. New York, NY: Oxford University Press.

Gero, A., K. Meheux, and D. Dominey-Howes. 2011. "Integrated Community Based Disaster Risk Reduction and Climate Change Adaptation: Examples from the Pacific." *Natural Hazards and Earth System Sciences* 11, pp. 101–13.

GOB (Government of Bangladesh). 2009a. *Disaster Risk Reduction in Bangladesh, Best Practices*. Dhaka, Bangladesh: Disaster Management Bureau, Ministry of Food and Disaster Management, Government of Bangladesh.

GOB (Government of Bangladesh). 2009b. *Facilitators Guidebook practicing Gender & Social Inclusion in Disaster Risk Reduction*. Dhaka, Bangladesh: Directorate of Relief and Rehabilitation, Ministry of Food and Disaster Management, Government of Bangladesh.

GOB (Government of Bangladesh). 2010a. *Standing Orders on Disaster (SOD)*. Dhaka, Bangladesh: Disaster Management Bureau, Ministry of Food and Disaster Management, Government of Bangladesh.

GOB (Government of Bangladesh). 2010b. *Bangladesh National Plan for Disaster Management, 2010–2015*. Dhaka, Bangladesh: Department of Disaster Management, Ministry of Disaster Management and Relief, Government of Bangladesh.

GOB (Government of Bangladesh). 2012. *Disaster Management Act, 2012. Bangladesh Gazette, September 24, 2012*. Dhaka, Bangladesh: Department of Disaster Management, Ministry of Disaster Management and Relief, Government of Bangladesh.

GOB (Government of Bangladesh). 2015. *National Disaster Management Guidelines*. Dhaka, Bangladesh: Department of Disaster Management, Ministry of Disaster Management and Relief, Government of Bangladesh.

GOB (Government of Bangladesh). 2017. *Bangladesh National Plan for Disaster Management, 2016-2020* (Draft). Dhaka, Bangladesh: Department of Disaster Management, Ministry of Disaster Management and Relief, Government of Bangladesh.

Haque, M. 2000. "Indigenous Knowledge and Practices in Disaster Management in Bangladesh." In *Of Popular Wisdom: Indigenous Knowledge and Practices in Bangladesh,* eds. N. A. Khan and S. Sen, pp. 141–45. Dhaka, Bangladesh: Bangladesh Resource Centre for Indigenous Knowledge.

Haque, M. 2013. *Environmental Governance: Emerging Challenges for Bangladesh*. Dhaka, Bangladesh: AH Development Publishing House.

Haque, M. 2017. "Community Based Adaptation to Climate Change: Experience of the Coastline of Bangladesh." In *Culture, Adaptation and Resilience, Essays on Climate Change Regime in South Asia,* eds. Z. Islam, H. Shafie and R. Mahmood, pp. 173–87. Dhaka, Bangladesh: Bangladesh Climate Change Trust and Department of Anthropology, University of Dhaka.

Hassan, S. 2000. "Indigenous Perceptions, Predictions and Survival Strategies Concerning Cyclones in Bangladesh." In *Of Popular Wisdom: Indigenous Knowledge and Practices in Bangladesh,* eds. N. A. Khan and S. Sen, pp. 147–50. Dhaka, Bangladesh: Bangladesh Resource Centre for Indigenous Knowledge.

Hyogo (Hyogo Framework for Action). 2015. *International Strategy for Disaster Reduction, Building the Resilience of Nations and Communities to Disasters,* 2005–2015. www.unisdr.org/wcdr

Islam, A., and A. Sumon. 2013. "Integration of Climate Change Adaptation, Disaster Risk Reduction and Social Protection in Bangladesh: Contemporary Views and Experience." In *Disaster Risk Reduction: Methods, Approaches and Practices, Climate Change Adaption Actions in*

Bangladesh, eds. R. Shaw, F. Mallick, and A. Islam, pp. 71–89. Tokyo, Japan: Springer.

MoEF (Ministry of Environment and Forests). 2009a. *National Adaptation Programme of Action (NAPA)*. Dhaka, Bangladesh: Ministry of Environment and Forests, Government of Bangladesh.

MoEF (Ministry of Environment and Forests). 2009b. *Bangladesh Climate Change Strategy and Action Plan*. Dhaka, Bangladesh: Ministry of Environment and Forests, Government of Bangladesh.

Ministry of Disaster Management and Relief Bangladesh Secretariat. 2012. *Cyclone Shelter Construction, Maintenance and Management Policy*. Dhaka, Bangladesh: Ministry of Disaster Management and Relief Bangladesh Secretariat.

Nasreen, M. 2000. "Indigenous Coping Mechanisms: The Role of Rural Women during Non-Flood and Flood Periods." *Grassroots Voice* 3, no. 3, pp. 69–81.

Pandey, B., and K. Okazaki. 2005. "Community Based Disaster Management: Empowering Communities to Cope with Disaster Risks." Tokyo, Japan: United Nations Centre for Regional Development.

Reid, H., and E. L. F. Schipper. 2014. "Upscaling Community based Adaptation, An Introduction to the Edited Volume." In *Community-Based Adaptation to Climate Change, Scaling it up*, eds. E. L. F. Schipper, J. Ayers, H. Reid, S. Huq, and A. Rahman, pp. 3–21. Abingdon, UK: Routledge.

Task Force for Disaster, Community Readiness, and Recovery, The Society for Community Research and Action. 2010. *How to Help Your Community Recover from Disaster: A Manual for Planning and Action*. Macon, GA: Society for Community Research and Action.

United Nations (UN). 2014. *Progress and Challenges in Disaster Risk Reduction*. New York, NY: United Nations.

United Nations (UN). 2015. *Sendai Framework for Disaster Risk Reduction, 2015–2030*. New York, NY: United Nations.

Yodmani, S. 2001. "Disaster Risk Management and Vulnerability Reduction: Protecting the Poor." Paper delivered at the Social Protect Workshop 6: Protecting Communities—Social Funds and Disaster Management, Asia and Pacific Forum on Poverty: Reforming Policies and Institutions for Poverty Reduction, Manila, Asian Development Bank, February 5–9, 2001.

CHAPTER 4

Psychological Impact of Disasters

Discussion and Lessons from India

Gay Hui Ting Evelyn

School of Business, Singapore University of Social Sciences,
Singapore

Introduction

The experience of going through natural disasters can bring about psychological disorders such as post-traumatic stress disorder (Mason, Andrews, and Upton 2010). This results from a number of factors, such as loss of loved ones, property damage, and relocation (Neria, Nandi, and Galea 2008), loss of livelihood, lack of water, sanitation, and basic comforts following a disaster (Galea et al. 2008), physical pain, and emotional shock or terror. This chapter will discuss some of these factors resulting in psychological distress following a disaster, as well as the factors associated with higher likelihood of developing post-traumatic stress disorder.

The region of the Indian subcontinent is one of the most vulnerable regions in the world to the occurrence of disasters, both natural and man-made. This can be attributed to its unique geological conditions. Almost 85 percent of the country is susceptible to at least one type of threat (SAARC 2009). In a report by the National Institute of Disaster Management (NIDM) (2014), it was reported that 27 out of 36 states and union territories in India are vulnerable to disasters. Close to 58.6 percent of India's land is vulnerable to moderate or severe earthquakes, 12 percent of the land is vulnerable to floods and river erosion, and approximately 76 percent of India's coastline is susceptible to cyclones and tsunamis. India is also highly susceptible to drought, landslides, and avalanches (National Institute of Disaster Management 2014).

Research has shown that the psychological impact of natural disasters is greater on survivors in developing countries than those in developed countries, and this may be explained by the severity of the disasters experienced by the people in developing countries, and their struggle to recover in the context of a lack of resources (Norris et al. 2002). Hence, this chapter looks at examples of disasters that happened in India, which is a developing country whose residents have lived through many disasters. In addition, it is interesting to examine the psychological impact of disasters in the context of India as many people in India suffer from psychological disorders. In fact, the President of India, Ram Nath Kovind warned that India is facing a "possible mental health epidemic" (The Hindu 2017), with almost 10 percent of the population suffering from some type of psychological disorders. In terms of absolute numbers, the number of Indians suffering from psychological problems is "larger than the entire population of Japan" (The Hindu 2017). In an article in *Wall Street Journal*, based on research by the risk analysis and research company Verisk Maplecroft, India was ranked as a country which has one of the largest number of people who are vulnerable to natural disasters. In fact, it was reported that 82 percent of the population in India are exposed to natural disasters, compared with 50 percent of the population in China (Abrams 2016).

In this chapter, I will present the research findings from the literature about the psychological disorders that result from disasters, and the factors that increase the likelihood of developing psychological issues. While we often think of the survivors and their family members as the victims who are vulnerable to developing mental disorders, disasters also affect the mental health of humanitarian aid workers. I draw examples from India as India is a country that has suffered multiple disasters, and a significant proportion of the population suffer from mental disorders. This chapter concludes by considering the importance of providing psychological support and counselling to sufferers.

Psychological Impact of Disasters

Post-traumatic Stress Disorder

Post-traumatic stress disorder has been found to be the most common type of psychological disorder that is experienced following exposure to a disaster (American Psychiatric Association, 2000; Neria, Nandi, and Galea 2008). Post-traumatic stress disorder is a serious condition, and its symptoms include flashbacks or nightmares regarding the disaster, negative changes in mood, emotional numbing, avoidance of triggers that remind them of the disaster, self-destructive behavior, and sleep disturbances (American Psychiatric Association 2000). Post-traumatic stress disorder can result from first-hand experience of the disaster, witnessing others experiencing the disaster, knowing that a loved one experienced a disaster, and being exposed to the effects of the disaster (such as rescue workers) (American Psychiatric Association 2013).

According to the American Psychiatric Association (2013), symptoms of post-traumatic stress disorder include repetitive memory of the traumatic event, repetitive dreams about the traumatic event, flashbacks about the event, and distress when they encounter cues associated with the traumatic event. As a result, the individual may avoid cues that remind them about the traumatic event.[1]

Post-traumatic Stress Disorder Following the Uttarakhand Flood

In June 2013, heavy rainfall and cloudburst triggered floods and landslides in the state of Uttarakhand. This was a disaster that caused extensive damage to infrastructure and loss of lives. It was described as "one of the most devastating disasters in the recent past in the region" (Satendra et al. 2014, page vii).

Following the disaster, researchers found that 32.8 percent of adolescents at a high school in Uttarkashi district in the Uttarakhand state

---

[1]The *Diagnostic and Statistical Manual of Mental Disorders* by the American Psychiatric Association is the result of an in-depth and broad review of the literature, secondary analyses, professional presentations, and discussions among experts (Pai, Suris, and North 2017).

exhibited probable signs of post-traumatic stress disorder (Nisha, Kiran, and Joseph 2014). A research study that looked at survivors from the districts of Uttarkashi, Tehri, and Pauri Garhwal 1 year after the flood found that among individuals who suffered loss attributable to the disaster (financial loss or loss of family member), 70.93 percent of those studied demonstrated symptoms of post-traumatic stress disorder. This suggests that the effects of experiencing a traumatic event due to natural disaster is persistent, and post-traumatic stress disorder symptoms are long-lasting (Srivastava et al. 2015). Interestingly, this study found that post-traumatic stress disorder symptoms were more common among people living in Tehri, where people were less affected by the disaster initially, than those living in Uttarkashi and Pauri. This is surprising since the extent of human loss of lives as a result of the Uttarakhand flood was less severe in the Tehri district as compared to Uttarkashi and Pauri. However, Tehri did experience destruction of the infrastructure and its economy. According to Srivastava et al. (2015), efficient repair and reconstruction in the Uttarkashi and Pauri districts helped to support the economy, which may have mitigated the psychological impact on the residents and helped them cope with the disaster. Srivastava et al. (2015) conclude that we may infer that following a disaster, victims whose initial exposure is less severe may turn out to be more susceptible to developing post-traumatic stress disorder because they fear that the disaster will recur. Hence, we should not neglect the mental health implications of a disaster on people with lower initial exposure to the event, and they should also be provided with post-disaster support.

Those who survive a disaster are often permanently scarred by the traumatic event. A survivor of the Uttarakhand floods recalled that when the disaster struck, she and her family members took shelter under a mountain, which was swarmed by a large crowd of people, which resulted in a stampede. She saw with her own eyes how her husband was crushed. With tears rolling down her eyes, she said, "My husband was gasping for breath and in front of my eyes I saw him breathing his last" (Pande 2013). After carrying her husband's body for the next 2 days, the survivor and her family had no choice but to perform his last rites and cremate his body, as the family could not get help and carrying the body around made survival difficult (Pande 2013). Another article recounts the experience of a 13-year-old survivor, who ate from garbage cans after starving for over 43 hours. Others experienced sleeping on dead bodies and witnessing their family members being washed away by the raging flood (The Health Site 2013). Survivors of a disaster can experience survivor's guilt. This is characterized by recurring thoughts about things that the person could have or should have done but did not, despite having no responsibility for the outcome of the disaster (Sherman 2011).

While most research has looked at the psychological implications of disasters on residents of the area where the disaster took place, even tourists who return home after the event, and who thus are spared from long-term problems with lack of sanitation and food, are vulnerable to developing post-traumatic stress disorder. In a study examining tourists who have returned home after experiencing the 2004 Indian Ocean tsunami, the authors found that a significant percentage of the survivors (16.8 percent) exhibited symptoms of post-traumatic stress disorder, even two and a half years after the disaster. Hence, there is a need to identify individuals who are more susceptible to developing post-traumatic stress disorder, and provide treatment for them (Kraemer et al. 2009).

Factors Associated with the Propensity to Develop Post-traumatic Stress Disorder

Gender

Research has generally found that women have a higher propensity to develop post-traumatic stress disorder than men do (Lee and Young 2001; Galea, Nandi, and Vlahov 2005; Galea et al. 2008). In the study by Srivastava et al. (2015) discussed above, the authors also find evidence that post-traumatic stress disorder symptoms were more prevalent among females than males in Tehri, Uttarkashi, and Pauri following the Uttarakhand flood. A study by Channaveerachari et al. (2015) also found that the proportion of females having psychological disorders is higher than that of males following the Uttarakhand disaster.

Age

Prior research has found that children and adolescents are more vulnerable to developing psychological disorders than adults are (Mason, Andrews, and Upton 2010). The study by Nisha, Kiran, and Joseph (2014) found that 32.8 percent of adolescents at a high school in the Uttarkashi district affected by the Uttarakhand flood showed signs of post-traumatic stress disorder even 3 months after the disaster. Similarly, a study by Aneelraj et al. (2016) found that following the Uttarakhand flood, 18 percent of children and adolescents in the Uttarkashi district of Uttarakhand exhibited signs of psychological distress.

Research has found that compared to young people, the elderly were more susceptible to developing post-traumatic stress disorder in the aftermath of a disaster. Indeed, Jia et al. (2010) found that following a disaster, the elderly had a significantly higher propensity of developing post-traumatic stress disorder symptoms than young adult survivors do. Pekovic et al. (2007) posit that this may be attributable to the heightened sense of helplessness experienced by the elderly due to their weaker health, weaker cognitive ability, and impaired sensory awareness.

Another study looked at the effect of the 2004 Indian Ocean tsunami on elderly survivors. The 2004 Indian Ocean tsunami was caused by a 9.1 magnitude earthquake that triggered huge waves in countries in South Asia and Southeast Asia. This resulted in huge devastation and at least 225,000 people losing their lives. It was reported that tens of thousands had died or were missing in Sri Lanka and India (Encyclopaedia Britannica 2008). In India alone, 10,273 people lost their lives, and 5,832 people were missing (Ministry of Home Affairs 2005). There was much devastation in the Andaman and Nicobar Islands, affecting the states of Tamil Nadu and Kerala, and the union territory of Pondicherry. The state of Andhra Pradesh was also moderately affected (Murty et al. 2006).

Viswanath et al. (2012) compared the psychological conditions of the elderly versus the younger adults during the first 3 months following the Indian Ocean tsunami in the Andaman and Nicobar Islands in India. The authors found that the elderly survivors exhibited more signs of adjustment disorder than the younger adults. Among survivors who remained in their own habitats after the disaster, the elderly displayed more signs of post-traumatic stress disorder. Among the elderly, those who remained in their own habitats showed more symptoms of adjustment disorder, and those who were displaced showed more signs of depression and anxiety disorders (Viswanath et al. 2012).

Other Individual Characteristics

Prior research has found that survivors' personality traits, in particular, neuroticism, is related to the likelihood of developing post-traumatic stress disorder (Galea, Nandi, and Vlahov 2005; Skogstad et al. 2013). In addition, the higher the victim's exposure to the disaster, the more severe the intensity of post-traumatic stress disorder symptoms he or she experiences (Briere and Elliott 2000), with extent of injury and personal threat to safety as stronger predictors of the severity of the psychological distress experienced (Maes et al. 2000). The survivors' preexisting mental health condition is also related to the severity of the psychological outcomes (Bromet et al. 1982). In other words, those who have prior psychiatric problems were more likely to suffer psychological issues following the occurrence of disasters.

It has also been found that those in the ethnic minority within India tend to suffer more severe psychological consequences (La Greca, Silverman, and Wasserstein 1998), in part because they are more likely to attribute the occurrence of disasters to external factors (such as the will of God) beyond their control, and face more stress owing to their minority status and the feeling of being marginalized (Perilla, Norris, and LaVizzo 2002, Norris et al. 2002). This implies that victims of the ethnic minority within the states of India who survive disasters may require more attention and counselling.

Post-traumatic Stress Disorder Suffered by Humanitarian Workers

Humanitarian workers are exposed to primary trauma resulting from physical danger to their safety, and secondary trauma resulting from witnessing others' suffering. Hence, compared to the average person, humanitarian relief workers have a higher propensity of suffering from post-traumatic stress disorder (Connorton et al. 2012). Prior research has looked at post-traumatic stress disorder and depression among rescue and response workers. Research has found that post-traumatic stress disorder symptoms are present in up to 34 percent of rescue and response workers, and depression present in up to 53 percent of these workers (Gabern, Ebbeling, and Bartel 2016). Symptoms exhibited by first responders and rescue workers include intrusive memories and avoidance of stimuli that remind them of the traumatic event (Skogstad et al. 2016). A study has found that following the 2001 World Trade Centre terror attacks, approximately 12 percent of firefighters and emergency medical personnel and 6 percent of police officers exhibited symptoms of post-traumatic stress disorder (Perrin et al. 2007).

First, relief workers are removed from their comfort zone and do not have access to the usual psychological support and social support of their family members. This results in stress, which heightens the possibility of developing post-traumatic stress disorder, depression, or anxiety. Second, and importantly, relief workers witness death and suffering, which is very traumatizing (Connorton et al. 2012). In the 1995 National Comorbidity Survey, it was found that witnessing the death or serious injury of a fellow human being was the most serious trauma for 24.3 percent of the men suffering from post-traumatic stress disorder (Kessler et al. 1995).

Factors that increase rescue workers' likelihood of experiencing post-traumatic stress disorder include increased exposure to the disaster, provision of assistance to the victims, lack of resources (Declercq et al. 2011), and threat to personal safety (Ozer et al. 2003). Research also found that post-traumatic stress disorder symptoms were more prevalent among untrained volunteers as compared to trained, professional rescue workers (Hagh-Shenas et al. 2005; Dyregrov, Kristoffersen, and Gjestad 1996).

While we may think that rescue workers who witness the scenes of the disaster and see death first hand are the ones most vulnerable to suffering from post-traumatic stress disorder, humanitarian aid workers who do not witness death nor witness the disaster scene first hand are also vulnerable, as they are exposed to secondary traumatic stress. Secondary traumatic stress results from indirect exposure to trauma, for instance, by listening to a story that recounts the traumatic event (Zimering, Munroe, and Gulliver 2003). People can be traumatized even without being personally harmed (American Psychiatric Association 2000). Prior studies have found that humanitarian aid workers who listen to victims' narratives recounting their pain and suffering are likely to be detrimentally affected psychologically and emotionally (Carbonell and Figley 1996).

Shah, Garland, and Katz (2007) define humanitarian aid workers as volunteers or employees who inquire details or provide care to those who suffered trauma. As a result of their work, they may suffer from nightmares and sleep disturbances (Figley 1995).

The Way Forward

It is important to conduct screening to detect post-traumatic stress disorder symptoms, and provide sufferers with social support, mental health, and counselling services (Sajid 2007). Prior research has demonstrated that receiving social support helps mitigate the psychological trauma brought on by external factors (Bolin 1986, Hobfoll et al. 1990, Tyler and Hoyt 2000). Social support can come from simply having someone to talk to and having someone to turn to for help. It comes from relationships that provide victims with a sense of security (Tyler 2006). In India, efforts made to rebuild or build new social support networks have been made, such as through the formation of small groups in the community (Juvva and Rajendran 2000).

In India, the Bhopal disaster saw the first systematic effort made to provide psychological intervention to victims (Rao 2006). Providing aid while respecting the dignity of the victims is also important, as there are sensitivity issues involved. Gandevia (2000) cited the difficulty faced by the older people in accepting old clothes, as the village was relatively prosperous prior to the earthquake. This has implications on aid workers in that they need to demonstrate sensitivity in the way that they distribute relief supplies. Rao (2006) also identifies the importance of supporting survivors by helping to identify dead bodies. This is an important psychological intervention, because not being able to find the body of a loved one has psychological consequences for survivors, as India has a culture where performing funeral rites for one's loved ones is important (Rao 2006).

Over the years, the help rendered to victims following disasters has improved, and volunteers have increasingly been better able to provide sound psychological counselling and support to victims (Rao 2006). In a study looking at victims of the 1993 Marathwada earthquake, it found that 139 per 1,000 in the affected area have psychological issues even

8 years after the disaster, and at least 30 percent of the survivors continue to need mental health support (Oxfam India 2001). The physical wounds of survivors may have healed, but the psychological distress and trauma they suffer may take many more years to heal. They need care, assistance, and support to overcome the psychological distress they experience. Hence, there is a need for long-term community-based rehabilitation efforts and delivery of counselling and mental health support. Apart from support rendered to the victims, it is also important to provide training to rescue workers and humanitarian aid workers. Such training should go beyond technical training, but also training in how to manage emotional challenges and stress management. Rescue workers and humanitarian aid workers also need to be provided with social support and provided with early treatment for post-traumatic stress disorder symptoms (Skogstad et al. 2013).

Conclusion

The onset of disasters can have a significant impact on people, whether they are directly affected or not. Apart from the survivors' physical injuries, the unseen, psychological trauma that they suffer warrant even more attention. Apart from survivors who lived through physical pain, those who lost their loved ones suffer psychological trauma. In addition to the local population, tourists who encounter a natural disaster also suffer psychological trauma, and the effects last even after they return to their home country. Rescue workers are also psychologically scarred, having witnessed death, destruction, and scores of dead bodies and mutilated body parts. Even humanitarian aid workers who listen and provide counselling to survivors are vulnerable to indirect trauma.

To conclude, it is important to take into consideration the possibility that survivors of disasters will suffer post-traumatic stress disorder, even if the disaster happened long ago. The importance of screening to detect post-traumatic stress disorder symptoms, and the importance of providing sufferers social support as well as counselling services, cannot be over-emphasized. In addition, rescue workers and humanitarian aid workers are in the front line. They should be provided with training and with social support. Given their higher risk of developing post-traumatic stress disorder, they need to be screened for the presence of post-traumatic stress disorder symptoms, so that early treatment can be provided.

References

Abrams, C. 2016. "How Prone Is India to Disaster?" *The Wall Street Journal.* https://blogs.wsj.com/indiarealtime/2016/03/28/how-prone-is-india-to-disaster

American Psychiatric Association. 2000. *Diagnostic and Statistical Manual of Mental Disorders DSM-IV-TR.* 4th ed. Washington, DC: American Psychiatric Association.

American Psychiatric Association. 2013. *Diagnostic and Statistical Manual of Mental Disorders.*5th ed. Arlington, VA: American Psychiatric Association.

Aneelraj, D., C. N. Kumar, R. Somanathan, D. Chandran, S. Joshi, P. Paramita, S. Kasi, R. Bangalore, and S. Math. 2016. "Uttarakhand Disaster 2013: A Report on Psychosocial Adversities Experienced by Children and Adolescents." *The Indian Journal of Pediatrics* 83, no. 4, pp. 316–21.

Bolin, R. C. 1986. "Disaster Characteristics and Psychosocial Impacts." In *Disasters and Mental Health: Contemporary Perspectives and Innovations in Services to Disaster Victims*, eds. B. J. Sowder and M. Lystad, pp. 11–35. Washington, DC: American Psychiatric Press.

Briere, J., and D. Elliott. 2000. "Prevalence, Characteristics, and Long-Term Sequelae of Natural Disaster Exposure in the General Population." *Journal of Traumatic Stress* 13, no. 4, pp. 661–79.

Bromet, E., Parkinson, D., Schulberg, H., Dunn, L., and Gondek, P. 1982. "Mental Health of Residents near the Three Mile Island Reactor: A Comparative Study of Selected Groups." *Journal of Preventive Psychiatry* 1, no. 3, pp. 225–76.

Carbonell, J. L., and C. R. Figley. 1996. "When Trauma Hits Home: Personal Trauma and the Family Therapist." *Journal of Marital and Family Therapy* 22, no. 1, pp. 53–58.

Channaveerachari, N. K., A. Raj, S. Joshi, P. Paramita, R. Somanathan, D. Chandran, and S. B. Math. 2015. "Psychiatric and Medical Disorders in the after Math of the Uttarakhand Disaster: Assessment,

Approach, and Future Challenges." *Indian Journal of Psychological Medicine* 37, no. 2, pp. 138–43.

Connorton, E., M. J. Perry, D. Hemenway, and M. Miller. 2012. "Humanitarian Relief Workers and Trauma-related Mental Illness." *Epidemiologic Reviews* 34, no. 1, pp. 145–55.

Declercq, F., R. Meganck, J. Deheegher, and H. Van Hoorde. 2011. "Frequency of and Subjective Response to Critical Incidents in the Prediction of PTSD in Emergency Personnel." *Journal of Traumatic Stress* 24, no. 1, pp. 133–36.

Dyregrov, A., J. Kristoffersen, and R. Gjestad. 1996. "Voluntary and Professional Disaster-workers: Similarities and Differences in Reactions." *Journal of Traumatic Stress* 9, no. 3, pp. 541–55.

Encyclopaedia Britannica. 2008. *Indian Ocean Tsunami of 2004.* https://www.britannica.com/event/Indian-Ocean-tsunami-of-2004

Figley, C. R. 1995. "Compassion Fatigue as Secondary Traumatic Stress Disorder: An Overview." In *Compassion Fatigue: Coping with Secondary Traumatic Stress Disorder*, ed. C. R. Figley, pp. 1–20. New York, NY: Brunner/Mazel.

Gabern, S. C., L. G. Ebbeling, and S. A. Bartel. 2016. "A Systematic Review of Health Outcomes among Disaster and Humanitarian Responders." *Prehospital and Disaster Medicine* 31, no. 6, pp. 635–42.

Gandevia, K. 2000. "Killari: Psychosocial Health of a Village Ravaged by an Earthquake." *The Indian Journal of Social Work* 61, no. 4, pp. 652–63.

Galea, S., A. Nandi, and D. Vlahov. 2005. "The Epidemiology of Post-traumatic Stress Disorder after Disasters." *Epidemiologic Reviews* 27, no. 1, pp. 78–91.

Galea, S., M. Tracy, F. Norris, and S. F. Coffey. 2008. "Financial and Social Circumstances and the Incidence and Course of PTSD in Mississippi During the First Two Years after Hurricane Katrina." *Journal of Traumatic Stress* 21, no. 4, pp. 357–68.

Hagh-Shenas, H., M. A. Goodarzi, G. Dehbozorgi, and H. Farashbandi. 2005. "Psychological Consequences of the Bam Earthquake on Professional and Nonprofessional Helpers." *Journal of Traumatic Stress* 18, no. 5, pp. 477–83.

Hobfoll, S. E., J. Freedy, C. Lane, and P. Geller. 1990. "Conservation of Social Resources: Social Support Resource Theory." *Journal of Social and Personal Relationships* 7, no. 4, pp. 465–78.

Jia, Z., W. Tian, W. Liu, Y. Cao, J. Yan, and Z. Shun. 2010. "Are the Elderly More Vulnerable to Psychological Impact of Natural Disaster? A Population-based Survey of Adult Survivors of the 2008 Sichuan Earthquake." *BMC Public Health* 10, pp. 172.

Juvva, S., and Rajendran, P. 2000. "Disaster Mental Health: A Current Perspective." *The Indian Journal of Social Work* 61, no. 4, pp. 527–41.

Kessler, R. C, A. Sonnega, E. Bromet, M. Hughes, and C. B. Nelson. 1995. "Posttraumatic Stress Disorder in the National Comorbidity Survey." *Archives of General Psychiatry* 52, no. 12, pp. 1048–60.

Kraemer, B., L. Wittmann, J. Jenewein, and U. Schnyder. 2009. "2004 Tsunami: Long-Term Psychological Consequences for Swiss Tourists in the Area at the Time of the Disaster." *Australian & New Zealand Journal of Psychiatry* 43, no. 5, pp. 420–25.

La Greca, A. M., W. K. Silverman, and S. B. Wasserstein. 1998. "Children's Predisaster Functioning as a Predictor of Posttraumatic Stress following Hurricane Andrew." *Journal of Consulting and Clinical Psychology* 66, no. 6, pp. 883–92.

Lee, D., and K. Young. 2001. "Post-traumatic Stress Disorder: Diagnostic Issues and Epidemiology in Adult Survivors of Traumatic Events." *International Review of Psychiatry* 13, pp. 150–58.

Maes, M., J. Mylle, L. Delmeire, and C. A. Altamura. 2000. "Psychiatric Morbidity and Comorbidity Following Accidental Man-made Traumatic Events: Incidence and Risk Factors." *European Archives of Psychiatry and Clinical Neuroscience* 250, pp. 156–62.

Mason, V., H. Andrews, and D. Upton. 2010. "The Psychological Impact of Exposure to Floods." *Psychology, Health & Medicine* 15, no. 1, pp. 61–73.

MHA (Ministry of Home Affairs). 2005. *Annual Report 2004–2005.* New Delhi, India: Government of India.

Murty, C. V. R., S. K. Jain, A. R. Sheth, A. Jaiswal, and S. R. Dash. 2006. "Response and Recovery in India after the December 2004 Great Sumatra Earthquake and Indian Ocean Tsunami." *Earthquake Spectra* 22, no. S3, pp. S731–58.

NIDM (National Institute of Disaster Management). 2014. *India*. nidm. gov.in/easindia2014/err/pdf/country_profile/India.pdf

Neria, Y., A. Nandi, and S. Galea. 2008. "Post-traumatic Stress Disorder Following Disasters: A Systematic Review." *Psychological Medicine* 38, no. 4, pp. 467–80.

Nisha, C., P. Kiran, and B. Joseph. 2014. "Assessment of Post-traumatic Stress Disorder among Disaster Affected Children in a High School in Uttarkashi District, Uttarakhand, India." *International Journal of Health System and Disaster Management* 2, no. 4, pp. 237–240.

Norris, F. H., M. J. Friedman, P. J. Watson, C. M. Byrne, E. Diaz, and K. Kaniasty. 2002. "60,000 Disaster Victims Speak: Part I. An Empirical Review of the Empirical Literature, 1981–2001." *Psychiatry: Interpersonal and Biological Processes* 65, no. 3, pp. 207–39.

Oxfam India. 2001. *Gujarat Earthquake: Healing the Wounds-Rapid Need Assessment Report & Long-term Intervention Strategy*. https://reliefweb .int/report/india/gujarat-earthquake-healing-wounds-rapid-need-assessment-report-long-term-intervention

Ozer, E. J., S. R. Best, T. L. Lipsey, and D. S. Weiss. 2003. "Predictors of Posttraumatic Stress Disorder and Symptoms in Adults: A Metaanalysis." *Psychological Bulletin* 129, no. 1, pp. 52–73.

Pai, A., A. M. Suris, and C. S. North. 2017. "Posttraumatic Stress Disorder in the *DSM-5*: Controversy, Change, and Conceptual Considerations." *Behavioural Sciences* 7, no. 1, p. 7.

Pande, A. 2013. "Uttarakhand Survivor Tales: 'Saw My Husband Die in Front of Me'." *Firstpost*. https://www.firstpost.com/india/uttarakhand-survivor-tales-saw-my-husband-die-in-front-of-me-898193.html

Pekovic V, L. Seff, and M. B. Rothman. 2007. "Planning for and Responding to Special Needs of Elders in Natural Disasters." *Generations* 31, no. 4, pp. 37–41.

Perrin, M. A., L. DiGrande, K. Wheeler, L. Thorpe, M. Farfel, and R. Brackbill. 2007. "Differences in PTSD Prevalence and Associated Risk Factors among World Trade Center Disaster Rescue and Recovery Workers." *American Journal of Psychiatry* 164, no. 9, pp. 1385–94.

Perilla, J. L., F. H. Norris, and E. A. LaVizzo. 2002. "Ethnicity, Culture, and Disaster Response: Identifying and Explaining Ethnic Differences in PTSD Six Months after Hurricane Andrew." *Journal of Social and Clinical Psychology* 21, no. 1, pp. 20–45.

Rao, K. 2006. "Lessons Learnt in Mental Health and Psychosocial Care in India after Disasters." *International Review of Psychiatry* 18, no. 6, pp. 547–52.

SAARC Disaster Management Centre. 2009. *India Disaster Knowledge Network (IDKN).* http://www.saarc-sadkn.org/countries/india/disaster_profile.aspx

Sajid, M. S. 2007. "Unearthing the Most Vulnerable: Psychological Impact of Natural Disasters." *The European Journal of Psychiatry* 21, no. 3, pp. 230–31.

Satendra, A. K. Gupta, V. K. Naik, T. K. Saha Roy, A. K. Sharma, and M. Dwivedi. 2014. *Uttarakhand Disaster 2015.* New Delhi, India: National Institute of Disaster Management. http://nidm.gov.in/books.asp

Shah, S. A., E. Garland, and C. Katz. 2007. "Secondary Traumatic Stress: Prevalence in Humanitarian Aid Workers in India." *Traumatology* 13, no. 1, pp. 59–70.

Sherman, N. 2011. "The Moral Logic of Survivor Guilt." *Psychology Today.* https://www.psychologytoday.com/us/blog/stoic-warrior/201107/the-moral-logic-survivor-guilt

Skogstad, M., M. Skorstad, A. Lie, H. S. Conradi, T. Heir, and L. Weisµth. 2013. "Work-related Post-traumatic Stress Disorder." *Occupational Medicine* 63, no. 3, pp. 175–82.

Skogstad, L., T. Heir, E. Hauff, and Ø. Ekeberg. 2016. "Post-traumatic Stress among Rescue Workers after Terror Attacks in Norway." *Occupational Medicine* 66, no. 7, pp. 528–35.

Srivastava, M., D. Goel, J. Semwal, R. Gupta, and M. Dhyani. 2015. "Post-traumatic Stress Disorder Symptoms in the Population of Uttarkashi, Tehri, and Pauri Garhwal India in Reference to Uttarakhand Flood-June 2013." *International Journal of Health System and Disaster Management* 3, no. 5, pp. 37–43.

The Health Site. 2013. *Uttarakhand Floods: Victims Suffering from Post-Traumatic Stress Disorder.* http://www.thehealthsite.com/news/uttarakhand-floods-victims-suffering-from-post-trauma-stress-disorder

The Hindu. 2017. *India Is Facing a Possible Mental Health Epidemic, Says President.* http://www.thehindu.com/news/national/karnataka/india-is-facing-a-possible-mental-health-epidemic-says-president/article22335971.ece

Tyler, K. A. 2006. "The Impact of Support Received and Support Provision on Changes in Perceived Social Support among Older Adults." *The International Journal of Aging and Human Development* 62, no. 1, pp. 21–38.

Tyler, K. A., and D. Hoyt. 2000. "The Effects of an Acute Stressor on Depressive Symptoms among Older Adults: The Moderating Effects of Social Support and Age." *Research on Aging* 22, no. 2, pp. 143–64.

Viswanath, B., A. S. Maroky, S. B. Math, J. P. John, V. Benegal, A. Hamza, and S. K. Chaturvedi. 2012. "Psychological Impact of the Tsunami on Elderly Survivors." *The American Journal of Geriatric Psychiatry* 20, no. 5, pp. 402–07.

Zimering, R., Munroe, J., and Gulliver, S. B. 2003. "Secondary Traumatization in Mental Health Care Providers." *Psychiatric Times 20*, no. 4, pp. 43–47.

CHAPTER 5

Engendering Disaster Risk Reduction at Grassroots Level

Neena Joseph

Independent Researcher
Kerala, Kochi, India

Introduction

Disaster risk reduction (DRR) is the crucial aspect of disaster management (DM). Global experience and research evince that hazards have disproportionally a more disastrous impact on women. Higher vulnerability and lesser coping capacity arising out of societally ordained lower position in the gender hierarchy lends partial explanation for this disparity. Hence, risk reduction initiatives, which are gender inclusively designed and implemented, would be inherently covering the risk reduction requirements of the general population. A comprehensive discussion considering the ground realities of politics, ethics, civic sense of the community, participation of vulnerable groups, inclusion of women and children, is needed before choosing a project for implementation vis-à-vis its alternatives. A framework for discussion around which all the relevant factors are put on the table by all the stakeholders and the alternatives are considered jointly and transparently, would be very useful. SWOT analysis can be used to mainstream gender concerns into the discussions.

Global and national policies advocate DRR, capacity building, multi stakeholder participation and participation of the community, especially that of vulnerable groups, and gender inclusiveness. "Paradigm shift" has happened from relief-centric response to proactive "prevention, mitigation and preparedness" driven approach (GOI 2009, p. 1). From the Hyogo Framework for Action (2005 to 2015) to the Sendai Framework for Disaster Risk Reduction (2015 to 2030); this shift is visible. The subject of this chapter is related to the "Sustainable Development Goals (SDGs): good health and well-being; gender equality; clean water and sanitation; decent work and economic growth; sustainable cities and communities and climate action" (Goals 3, 5, 6, 8, 11 and 13, respectively) (UNDP 2015, p. 18). For the success of DRR endeavors, the future international frameworks need to emphasize and highlight the active participation of the local community to a higher degree, than that done in the Sendai and Hyogo Frameworks (Tozier 2015). India's National Policy highlights making use of "corporate social responsibility (CSR), Public Private Participation (PPP)" (p. 21), and utilizing the resources of "National Cadet Corps (NCC), National Service Scheme (NSS), Nehru Yuva Kendra Sangathan" (p. 14). Coordination with "civil society" (p. 20), "techno legal and techno financial regimes" (pp. 23–24) is mentioned, capacity development (p. 37), training of communities (p. 34), knowledge management through sharing and dissemination of good practices (pp. 35–36) are spelled out as necessary means for effective DM (GOI 2009). The relevant national act of India has made it statutory to institute "national, state and district level disaster management authorities" (GOI 2005, p. 3). Twenty-three countries proposed the resolution "Gender Equality and Empowerment of women in Natural Disasters" during the 58th session of the Commission on Status of Women on March 2014. This evidences the significance of addressing the gender-specific vulnerabilities of women and girls and of realizing their partnership throughout the entire cycle of DM viz. "prevention, response and reconstruction" (UNESC 2014, p. 3).

The objectives of this chapter are to identify the problems faced by women in a disaster-prone area and to assess, at the grassroots level, the technological alternative for DRR that can enable women's participation, solve their disaster-related problems, and reduce their vulnerabilities.

Literature Review

The link between natural hazards, people's vulnerability, and disasters is explicated by Wisner et al. (2003). There is strong link between children's education and sustainable development. Children need to be educated in the sustainability of our planet. Eco literacy and critical thinking skills need to be developed in the future generation. (Wagner 2016). There are more poor women than poor men. Women's predominant presence in informal jobs, underpayment to women, skewed succession laws, gender unfriendly customs and overreliance on male family members result in powerlessness and lack of access and control over resources. They stay tethered to home due to the gender division of labor and this restricts their access to politics and other economic and educational opportunities (Anderson 1994). "Gender related vulnerability is deep rooted in persistent inequalities" (Enarson 2000, p. 5). Women's decision-making capacities are hampered due to the entrenched inequality. Risk of disasters are not homogeneously distributed among citizens. There is a gender effect in risk distribution (Enarson 2000). Disasters have more devastating impact on women (Enarson 2000). Women's workload intensifies during disasters (Enarson 2000). Women who live alone receive only late warning signals (Enarson 2000). Among women there are most vulnerable groups who require special care. Eighteen (18) categories of vulnerable groups of women were delineated including the poor, the senior, the ill, the homeless, the disabled, the abused, the recently migrated, the undocumented, the indigenous and those who are isolated and women who head families (Enarson 2000). The impact of disasters on pregnant women show that exposure to disasters resulted in an absence of prenatal care, an increase in morbidity, delivery of underweight babies, or a premature delivery (ACOG 2010). Higher the intensity of a disaster, particularly higher is the female mortality. The decline of life expectancy is higher for women than men consequent to a natural disaster. Again, this decline is comparatively higher for women belonging to lower economic strata. Hence a clear appreciation of the gendered nature of vulnerability and especially that of poor women is essential for all the stakeholders including the policy makers (Neumayer 2007). Investment in DRR will be paid back seven times in terms of avoidance of development losses. If women are understood to be much more vulnerable to disasters than men, then engendered DRR endeavors would make DRR and ultimately development, more efficient (Bradshaw 2013). If women and girls are considered as "vulnerable," their potential for DM will go unrecognized (Bradshaw 2013). The inherent strengths of women and girls need to be developed for efficacious DM. They need to participate in DRR as change agents (Bradshaw 2013). It is very important to accept community-based organizations (CBOs) as partners in DM (Enarson 2000).

During the contexts of the Great East Japan earthquake (2011); Fukushima nuclear disaster (2011); Sichuan earthquake in China (2008); Indian Ocean earthquake (2004); the four severe earthquakes in Mexico (from 2010 to 2012); typhoons, cyclones and landslides in New Zealand (from 2011) and the four earthquakes in Philippines (from 2010 to 2012), strong gender-sensitive interventions were made. Conversion of unremunerated domestic-level work to business opportunities, capacity building for entrepreneurship, setting up of botanical gardens, restoration of traditional handicrafts are a few examples. Involvement of local women, promoting community cohesion, forging of strategic partnerships etc. were common features in all these endeavors (SOM 2015).

The Area of Study and the Nature of Problem Faced by Women in This Area

The area of study is the Chellanam panchayat[1] in Ernakulam district, Kerala state, India (9.89° N Latitude and 76.26° E Longitude). The Chellanam Grama panchayat is selected for study because it is an eco-fragile and disaster-prone coastal panchayat. Chellanam is officially acknowledged as vulnerable as evidenced by its selection by District Disaster Management Authority (DDMA) for implementation of two World Bank projects: The National Cyclone Risk Mitigation Project and the Cyclone Shelter Project. It was also affected by the South Asian tsunami (2004). Funds are being planned for capacity development in this panchayat by DDMA. The problem of sea incursion in Ward 18 of Chellanam panchayat is taken

---

[1]Grama panchayats are the local bodies in rural area which are endowed with powers of local self-government through the 73rd Constitution Amendment Act 1992.

up for study. This is not a disaster, cataclysmic in nature, but an issue of perennial vexation for the past 10 years. Sea incursion occurs at high tides during three and a half months in a year causing formidable cleaning challenges and health threats for the community and more so for women. The reason is that cooking, cleaning, and caring are socially ordained as women's duties. Disasters of great magnitude in terms of intensity and spatial reach attract attention rather than small and medium disasters, even though the cumulative impact of the latter may be greater. Chellanam is a potential candidate for a disaster of huge scale.[2]

Currently, the problem is caused by just a 100-m gap in the rubble-mounted sea wall in the ward. This is a local problem, but a microscopic study unravels the ground-level dynamics in the context of larger issues beyond the scope of the panchayat. The high budget permanent solution of rubble-mounted sea wall is beyond the scope of the panchayat. At the time of study, the panchayat was seriously considering to put up geotextile protection walls (GTPW) in the gap.

The significance of the study lies in the suggestion of a workable and simple model for engendered discussion around the jurisdictionally feasible local-level project alternatives to solve local problems.

The chapter attempts to address the following questions:

A) What are the vulnerabilities of women in Ward 18 of Chellanam panchayat?
B) What are the gender-related issues for women in Ward 18 due to sea incursion?
C) What would be the appropriate technology to reduce the vulnerabilities of these women and to solve their problems?

GTPW Technology and Its Technological Alternatives

Bags (2 m × 1 m × 0.4 m) made of geo-synthetic unwoven UV-susceptible material (with petroleum base) are filled with water and sand from the worksite itself. The material will be densified as and when it is filled.

---

[2]A severe cyclonic storm Ockhi hit Kerala on 28th November 2017. Chellanam was affected.

Mechanized filling is more efficient (usually up to 1,100 kg) than manual filling (800 kg). Machines are used to stack the bags up to a height of 3.6 m or so according to the requirement of the pertinent spot. The "wall" is wrapped with geotextile and securely sewed up. Then, sand is piled behind the GTPW. The creeper, adambu[3] is planted in the sand behind the bags. As it grows, it crawls up the GTPW and into the front side of the wall and becomes a bio fence. Adambu consolidates the sand pile and bolsters up the geo bags. The approximate cost of this work is about Rs15 to 16 lakhs per 100 m (approximately US$22,000). The duration of the wall is 4 to 5 years. The wall is supposed to last from 4 to 5 years. GTPW is a relatively new technology. But the same technology had been applied 1 year ago in Purakkad beach in the Alappuzha district, Kerala, with a nearly 100-m-long protection wall. There are not many complaints. A costlier but more lasting alternative to GTPW is geo tube protection walls (GTbPW). The most lasting permanent solution is a rubble-mounted protection wall, which is the costliest alternative and which can be the most useful if a large-scale natural hazard occurs. A variation of GTPW, that is, Gj/cPW, is also in use where coir and jute are used instead of geothermal textile. The size of the tube is considerably larger when compared to the bags used in GTPW.[4] These technical details are collected from the records and pamphlets of the Irrigation Department, District Office, Ernakulam, Kerala and by interviewing the engineers of the department.

Research Methodology

The study was undertaken during August and September 2017. Secondary data was collected from the records and publications of Chellanam panchayat office. Key informants were interviewed including panchayat presidents[5] (current and previous), vice-president, CDS (Community

---

[3]Adambu is a type of creeper on which rabbits usually feed.

[4]These technical details were collected from the office of the Executive Engineer, Irrigation Division, Ernakulam District and by interviewing the Executive Engineer.

[5]Panchayat president heads each panchayat samithy (committee), which in turn is constituted by ward members. A panchayat is divided into wards and from each ward, a representative is elected to the panchayat samithy as ward member. In Kerala there are 941 panchayats. Chellanam panchayat has 22 wards.

Development Society) Chairperson,[6] Ward members, ADS chairpersons, neighborhood group members of Kudumbasree. Functionaries of Government of Kerala from various departments such as Irrigation, Coastal Engineering, Public Health, Revenue, Rural Development were interviewed. MGNREGS (Mahatma Gandhi National Rural Employment Guarantee Scheme) and DDMA functionaries helped with relevant information. Focus group discussions (FGDs) were conducted with Neighbourhood Group (NHG) members from Ward 18 and with previous and current ward members (see Table 5.1). The contemplated GTPW technology initiatives are then subjected to the SWOT analysis (strength, weakness, opportunity, and threat analysis) keeping in view the gender concerns and the alternatives of using coir/jute materials for the bags.

Table 5.1 Details of the FGDs

	FGD: NHG members	FGD—Current and former ward members
Date	Sept 7, 2017	Sept 12, 2017
Number of members	20	15

Source: Field Work.

The information about the issues and problems of women and their vulnerability was collected through FGDs with NHG members. Subsequently the discussions with ward members yielded information about the current realities of the bureaucratic dealings. Technical details related to construction were obtained from the engineers of the Irrigation Department. They also provided information related to the dealings with

---

[6]CDS Chairperson heads CDS, which is the local body level institution of Kudumbasree (literal meaning is prosperity of the family) launched in 1998 to eradicate poverty through community action under the leadership of local bodies. This is a three tier network with Area Society (ADS) at ward level and Neighbourhood Groups (NHG) s at grassroots level. In Kerala, grassroots democracy is facilitated through functional linkages with panchayats. As on March 2017, the system has 277,175 NHGs affiliated to 19,854 ADSs and 1,073 CDSs with a total membership of 4,306,976 women (Jawahar M). Chellanam panchayat has 21 ADSs, 320 NHGs with 4864 women as members.

the local body leaders and prominent citizens. The information collected from various sources were triangulated.

Technical details were collected from office of the Irrigation Department, Government of Kerala. Information about the Panchayat and Kudumbasree were collected from the respective websites, the references of which are given as CP (2017) and KS (2017) and supplemented with information from the relevant interviewees.

Scope and Limitation of the Study

This chapter attempts to bring out all the gender aspects within the panchayat, which need to be considered while choosing an appropriate DRR alternative. A SWOT framework is presented to bolster an engendered discussion and preliminary choice. This is a microscopic study. Only DRR alternatives, which is within the scope of the grassroots level are considered. The details of how women can learn about DM and DRR alternatives, how they can advocate their case in the panchayat through the CBOs, how to develop the advocacy skills and influence the powers to be for bringing a permanent solution that can withstand a major disaster is beyond the scope of this chapter. Rubble mounted walls can provide permanent solutions for major disasters. But this requires quarring which in turn can create ecological problems at the site of quarries. All these important aspects are beyond the scope of this study, but constitute useful subjects for future studies.

Conceptual Framework

Risk Reduction

A hazard is defined as

> a dangerous phenomenon, substance, human activity or condition that may cause loss of life, injury or other health impacts, property damage, loss of livelihoods and services, social and economic disruption, or environmental damage. (UNISDR 2009, p. 17)

There are natural hazards and human-made disasters. A disaster is

> a serious disruption of the functioning of a community or a society involving widespread human, material, or environmental losses

and impacts which exceeds the ability of the affected community to cope using only its own resources. (UNISDR 2009, p. 9)

"Risk is defined as the combination of the probability of an event and its negative consequences" (UNISDR 2009, p. 25). Thus, risk is associated with the degree to which humans cannot cope (lack of capacity) with a hazard.

Disaster Risk Reduction is defined as the concept and practice of reducing disaster risks through systematic efforts to analyze and manage the causal factors of disaster, including through reduced exposure to hazards, lessened vulnerability of people and property, wise management of land environment and improved prepared-ness for adverse effects. (UNISDR 2009, p. 10)

Hazard is the cause and/or trigger. A disaster is the result of a hazard's impact on society. The impact of a disaster is the result of a spectrum of many dynamic non hazard factors such as "physical, social, cultural and institutional." It depends on the profile of the individual defined by fac-tors of "class, caste, ethnicity, gender, age, disability" (Twigg 2001, p. 9). Hazards per se do not constitute disasters.

Vulnerability is defined as "the characteristics of a person or group and their situation that influence their capacity to anticipate, cope with, resist and recover from the impact of a natural hazard." The main determinants of vulnerability are "class, occupation, caste, ethnicity, gender, disability, health status, age, immigration status and the nature and extent of social networks." "Legal rights, access to physical and social networks, information" are also determinants (Wisner et al. 2003, pp. 11–12). Vulnerability is associated with lack of capability to prevent a hazard or manage its consequences (Wisner et al. 2003, pp. 13–14).

Disasters occur due to the interplay of hazard, vulnerability, and cop-ing capacity (UNISDR 2002, p. 15). This interaction is depicted as

Disaster risk (R) = Vulnerability (V) × Hazard (H)/Capacity (C)
(USAID 2011, p. 15).

SWOT Analysis

In a SWOT analysis not only the strengths and weaknesses (which are internal to an entity) but also the threats and opportunities (which are external to the entity) are discussed thoroughly. Thus, a SWOT framework if used in discussions can take the discussions beyond the tangible, immediate, and obvious factors of the entity that is subjected to analysis. When discussions are made using the SWOT framework, a lot of information is generated which will facilitate the decision-making to address the objectives of the entity and the pertinent social milieu (Morrison 2012). For example, a SWOT analysis can be performed on a community organization with the objective of comprehensively diagnosing the factors that can facilitate the implementation of a scheme. A SWOT can be performed on the same organization with another objective of assessing the suitability of diversifying into a new service. The first step in conducting a SWOT analysis discussion of the entity is: fixing the objective of the discussion. The next step is the exploration of "the internal and external attributes of the entity," which are helpful for the achievement of the objective (strengths and opportunities) or detrimental for the same (weaknesses and threats). Strengths and weaknesses are the current realities, while opportunities and threats future possibilities/probabilities (Morrison 2012). The external factors are the larger economic, technological, legal, social, cultural, and market-related in nature. Strategies are to be devised to use/build/leverage the strengths; stop/remedy/overcome the weaknesses; exploit/prioritize/capture/build/plan/manage the threats (Morrison 2016). Generation of comprehensive data and discussions around these open up many possibilities for conversion and matching. Weaknesses can be converted to strengths using opportunities. Threats can be converted to opportunities using strengths. Threats and weaknesses can be converted to strengths and opportunities (Team FME 2013). Strengths are matched to opportunities to gain competitive advantage. A SWOT analysis is a data capture process and is only the initial step toward the more in-depth analysis. A SWOT analysis is a simple and versatile tool. But it is subjective. What is classified as strength and weakness depends on the judgment (Team FME 2013) of the person/s concerned. A SWOT cannot be done effectively by just one person. It requires team effort (Morrison 2016). Although it is simple, oversimplification is to be avoided. Ideas are generated using brainstorming. Persons with vested interest might misrepresent strengths and weaknesses to their advantage (Team FME 2013). A SWOT aims at collecting and utilizing the knowledge about the "internal and external environment" for "strategy formulation" (Sammut-Bonnici and Galea 2015, p. 2). The objective of a SWOT analysis is to use the knowledge an organization has about its environment and to formulate its strategy accordingly (Sammut-Bonnici and Galea 2015).

Discussion and Findings

Issues Related to Sea Incursion

Sea incursion and water logging throw formidable challenges in the spheres of paddy, shrimp, and vegetable cultivations and also on health and sanitation. It is women who bear the brunt of all these impacts given their socially ordained roles of caring for the sick and based on the societal expectations to compromise their needs in the eventuality of a financial breakdown in the family.

Chellanam panchayat is situated in the southwestern part of the Ernakulam district with the Arabian Sea on the west and backwaters running from north to south on the eastern part. It is only 19.6-km long and 1-km wide. The fact that the area is only 1-km wide makes it more susceptible to the perils of sea incursion. The panchayat is on an average 30 cm below sea level seawards and 30 cm above sea level landwards. These geographical factors make the site eco-fragile.

Ward 18 is protected along the coast with sea walls made of granite rubble, but there is a gap of 100 m caused by damage to the sea wall. During high tides, episodes of sea incursion occur starting from the middle of May and last till the end of August. These episodes are unpredictable. During these months, episodes can happen during high tides commencing at any time from 11 a.m. to 10 p.m. There could be intermittent episodes also. In Ward 18, the houses are situated as close as 3 to 12 m from the sea. During high tides, the sea water rushes into the land through the gap flooding the already infirm terrain of loose soil. The water floods the courtyards and backyards of the houses bringing along with it sand and clay. Many of the houses and latrines happen to "sit" because the inundating waters carry away with it the sand under the floors of the houses. The water, clay, and waste enter the houses and create perpetual cleaning challenges to women, because cooking and cleaning are the roles set apart exclusively for them. The sea sometimes takes away in its sweep the utensils, coconut, and anything which lies on its way. The sea water damages the houses and there is the never-ending maintenance work consuming time, energy, and money of the citizens. The maximum amount obtained from Revenue department is only 5,000 and that too with inordinate delay of up to 1 year. Everything together makes house management a nightmare for women.

In the houses without septic tanks, with only ring-type latrines, as the water inundates the yards, the latrine waste seeps up. This generates an abominable health-threatening environment, causing the risk of waterborne diseases such as cholera, hepatitis A, and typhoid, which are acute diarrheal diseases.

Vijayam canal, the major canal constructed along the length of the panchayat, has inadequate depth and is ill maintained. The ducts and canals that are constructed to carry the flooded sea water from the western part of the panchayat to the backwaters in the eastern part eventually becomes silted up. A glance at the canals evidences the callousness and disregard for the maintenance of the canals and the indiscriminate waste dumping. Hence, it cannot contain the water that enters from the western part of the panchayat.

Culex mosquitoes, which breed in dirty water, serve as vectors of Japanese encephalitis, filariasis, etc. When there is any illness for anyone in the family, going by the socially constructed caring role of women, it is on the shoulders of women that the entire burden of the nursing of all family members falls. When the treatment expenses increase and consequently the non-health component of the family budget shrinks, it is on the women's needs that the budget cut ultimately happens. This situation has been prevailing since the last 10 years and the situation has exacerbated in the last 6 years.

Drinking water shortage is a perennial issue in the panchayat. The incursion of the sea and seepage of toilet waste together contaminate the quality of water in wells. Drinking water is brought in tanker lorries and from there it is pumped through pipes directly into the households. Water reaches every week or fortnight and each family gets about 350 to 400 L. The persons at the upper end (near the source of supply, i.e., the tanker) get more water and the quantity decreases progressively toward the lower ends.

The amount spent for preventing sea incursion in Chellanam village[7] is Rs 360,805 during the financial year 2016–2017. From the village, aid is given to the flood-affected persons. The maximum amount disbursed is Rs 5,000 and the average amount paid is in the range of Rs 2,500 to Rs 3,500. The system is so slow that none out of the 99 applicants had received compensation during the previous year.

Vulnerability of Women in the Panchayat

The sex ratio[8] is 1,009 in the panchayat. But literacy rate for women is only 91.4 percent whereas it is 93.47 percent for the entire panchayat (CP 2017). Detailed occupation-related data was obtained for Chellanam village. Ward 18 comes under Chellanam village and hence the data throw light on the dismal employment status of women there. Women comprise 22.86 percent of the total workforce. But they mainly fall into the category of marginal workers, constituting 77.43 percent of this category (DCO 2011). Information gathered through the FGDs and interviews revealed that most women are dependent on husbands and that their main type of work is going out to the nearest town of Kochi (approximately 25 km away) as domestic workers, in which case they do not get time for community-based activities. During the FGDs with NHG members and interviews with ward members, there was clear indication of male domination as evidenced by the prevalence of domestic violence, alcoholism, and the practice of dowry. About 68 percent of houses are not

---

[7]Village is the basic unit of division of land by Revenue department, whereas panchayat is the basic unit for the department of local self-government. Three villages lie within the boundary of Chellanam panchayat. They are Chellanam, Kumbalangi, and Rameswaram villages. Only Chellanam village is plagued by sea incursion.

[8]Sex ratio: The proportional distribution of the sexes in a population. Here it is expressed as the number of females per 1,000 male population.

solidly constructed, 20 percent of houses do not have sanitary facilities, and 6 percent of houses do not have safe drinking water (from files and discussions).

SWOT Analysis: GTPW

SWOT Analysis at a Glance

The analysis revolves round the objective of generating and classifying information to make a choice between the various technologies to prevent sea incursion. The objective is to facilitate the choice of a technology in which women can get remunerated, can participate, and can be involved in averting disasters in their own locality so as to reduce their vulnerability. At the time of the study, the panchayat was seriously contemplating the choice of GTPW technology in Ward 18. So, a SWOT analysis will be done from the vantage point of GTPW technology. Using a SWOT, facts related to the economic, technological, ecological, cultural, social, ethical, and administrative ecosystems are captured. Strengths and weakness of the project are examined based on ground-level realities. Missed opportunities are regarded. The facts beyond the tangible and direct aspects of costs and benefits and strengths and weaknesses are considered.

Here the entity under discussion is GTPW technology vis-à-vis its alternatives applied for the 100 m of sea coast in Ward 18 of Chellanam panchayat. Since the rubble-mounted protection wall and geo-tubes are beyond the scope and jurisdiction of the panchayat, the main discussion is in comparison with the variant of GTPW using coir and jute material.

The points at a glance are displayed in Table 5.2.

Strength

The filling material for GTPW is locally available sand and water. Hence all costs and problems associated with raw materials and transportation are avoided. The total cost per 100 m is Rs 15 to 20 lakhs (US$22,000 to 28,000) for GTPW, whereas it is Rs 57 lakhs (US$82,500) and 60 to 62 (US$87,000 to 90,000) lakhs, respectively, for geo-tubes and rubble-mounted walls. The ease and speed of implementation is comparatively

Table 5.2 SWOT analysis of GTPW (vis-à-vis the technological alternatives, especially the Gij/cPW alternatives)

Strength of GTPW	Weakness of GTPW
• Free availability of the filler material at site • Comparative inexpensiveness vis-à-vis rubble walls and geo tubes • Heaviness of bags prevents stealing • Speed of implementation and suitability as a quick solution • Avoidance of raw material scarce and procedurally cumbersome rubble technology, plagued with macro-level hurdles and ground-level petty goondaism* • Less supervision needed against vandalism and stealing	• New technology and hence not tried and tested • Not labor intensive in comparison with Gij/cPW • Not women-friendly technology when compared with Gij/cPW • Non-UV-resistant and hence not long-lasting when compared with the rubble-mounted wall and geo-tubes • Temporary solution only vis-à-vis rubble and geo-tube technology • Non-biodegradable material and hence has inherent environmental issues
Opportunity for Gij/cPW • Favorable global thinking, national policy, and national statute pivoted on community participation; roles of local governance and administration; gender equality, and capacity building • The area is already recognized as eco-fragile and there is already fund allocation for training and DRR activities **Opportunity (missed/unutilized if GTPW is chosen)** **Unutilized opportunities** • Organized and strong network of Kudumbasree and Balasabhas, which facilitate formation of vigilance groups and captive trainees • Robust MGNREGS set up • Power of panchayats in supervision against vandalism and stealing • Unemployed female labor force	**Threats (if GTPW is chosen over Gij/cPW is chosen)** • The material used in GTPW is not biodegradable and can harm the environment **Threats averted (if GTPW is chosen over Gij/cPW)** • The very much needed supervision getting diluted to the detriment of the Gij/cPW in the eventuality of local governance becoming inefficient and the CBO members becoming indifferent • Lack of adequate civic sense to sustain the project

(continued)

Table 5.2 SWOT analysis of GTPW (vis-à-vis the technological alternatives, especially the Gj/cPW alternatives) (continued)

Missed opportunities
- Not labor intensive. Hence missed opportunity to pump in MGNREGS funds to the local economy and for generating employment, mainly for women
- Missed opportunity to decrease the vulnerability of women through income generation
- Missed opportunity of participation of women and children in DRR-related community involvement and social action

Capacity Development and community action missed
- Opportunity for women to enter into DRR activities and to become partners to solve their perennial problem of sea incursion
- Acquisition of technical skills for women
- Gaining practical knowledge on DM and more specifically on DRR
- Eventual development of advocacy skills and bargaining skills to work toward more robust solutions beyond the scope of the panchayat
- Education of women and children on sustaining the environment and for developing civic sense
- Conscientization and training against vandalism
- Community mobilization for vigilance against theft and vandalism
- Training and R&D around DRR activities
- Offering leadership to inculcate civic sense and ethical operations
- Exploration of opportunities for repair work
- R&D to consolidate indigenous knowledge and to promote innovativeness

*Goondaism: Anti-social behavior of persons who generally indulge in violent and other illegitimate means to get things done.

more for GTPW while rubble technology is plagued with raw material scarcity, transportation hurdles, gawking charges, extortion from police, local leaders etc. GTPW is a temporary but quick solution to the problem of sea incursion. The heaviness of bags (1,100 kg) prevents stealing of sand whereas in the jute/coir alternative, probability of stealing is a negative aspect and hence the need for continued supervision is far less in comparison with Gj/cPW.

Weakness

Experience with GTPW is as short as 1 year, for example, Purakkad beach, Alappuzha district, Kerala. Though it was maintenance-free up to 1-year, longevity is unknown. Being[9] UV nonresistant, the material of the bag is at risk of damage and replacement. The material is not biodegradable whereas coir and jute used in Gj/cPW are perfectly biodegradable. The predicted life of GTPW is only 4 to 5 years against 10 years that of GTbPW. GTPW and GTbPW are temporary solutions. They cannot withstand cyclones like the rubble-mounted wall. This technology is machine-based unlike that of Gj/cPW, which is labor intensive. GTPW technology is not women friendly. Each bag weighs about 1,100 kg, approximating the weight of 22 cement sacks.

Threats

GTPW poses environmental problems since the material used is not biodegradable. In GTPW there is no threat for children and others to cause damages. Such type of vandalism had happened in Alleppey district with the Gj/cPW. Also, there is no threat of stealing the covering materials. The miscreants are usually those who own houses in the eastern parts or coastal areas and who encroach the sea shore (on the west) and put up houses with the sole objective of getting government aid. In short, the efficacy of Gj/cPW heavily depends on good governance related to timely repairs, vigilance, handling of miscreants, and civic sense education for the stakeholders including children. If there is ineffective leadership or

---

[9]Not resistant to ultra violet rays

lack of enthusiasm from the community, the sustainability of Gj/cPW will be at stake.

Opportunities

The global thinking, national legislation, and the national policy align with the concepts of DRR, community participation, partnership of women and children, involvement of local bodies and government, R&D, documentation of best practices, knowledge sharing and dissemination, public–private participation, capacity building, banking on corporate philanthropy etc. To prevent disaster in the making, when decision has to be taken at panchayat level, rubble-mounted technology may not feasible and so also the GTbPW (though theoretically it can be said that the panchayat can assert at higher level through lobbying and advocacy). So, the panchayat is left with the opportunity of choosing GTPW and its less sophisticated version, Gj/cPW.

The panchayat has a huge support system comprising of Kudumbasree with 4,864 women along with Balasabhas for children. Also, the panchayat has the MGNREGS scheme with a high potential for generating employment for eco-restorative activities. Female unemployment prevails in the panchayat as mentioned earlier. The closer supervision demanded by Gj/cPW is very well within the power of the panchayat. If Gj/cPW technology is chosen, we could utilize all these structures. The panchayat misses these opportunities if GTPW is chosen. Through MGNREGS, the panchayat can obtain funds from the state and central government if the panchayat opts for Gj/cPW. Choice of Gj/cPW can provide employment to the women within their locality and hence offers them more time for community participation. Choice Gj/cPW technology can reduce their vulnerability, not through wages alone, but also through the control women get over their environment by averting the damages caused by sea incursion through participation in both technological and community-based activities. Choice of Gj/cPW can make them active partners in R&D on substitution materials for the bags (through multi stakeholder groups including women who search for improvising indigenous knowledge). They can partner in civic sense education against vandalism and stealing and in other pertinent community actions along these lines. Literature shows that all these activities have reduced the vulnerability of women across the globe. Thus, many opportunities will be lost if GTPW technology is chosen.

DDMA has an allotment of Rs 5.9 lakhs (US$8,550) for training activities within the district. Training on technical aspects such as repair of bags and consciousness raising to promote civic sense can be undertaken. A heterogeneous team consisting of local people, leaders, academicians, community leaders, and engineers can visit sites where a range of technologies are used against sea incursion and an interested team can engage in R&D activities. Initiation into the construction activities through Gj/cPW could have given an entry to women into the world of DM and DRR. This could lay the foundation for skills, knowledge, and public action to know and think about alternate DRR activities and to negotiate and dialogue for other more robust alternatives. These skills could be taken further in due course to negotiate with the larger power centers to find permanent solutions even against large-scale disasters.

Scope can be explored for labor mobilization for repair work in the alternate technologies. The already existing Kudumbasree and Balasabhas can be mobilized for DRR projects. In Ward 18, there are 265 registered[10] job card holders and of those 210 are active out of which 95 percent are women. For the district, the figure is only 93 percent. But the average number of days of employment is only 30 days versus the district figure of 44. Many women go to cities for domestic work and the daily earnings is

---

[10]This is a national-level program in India, which guarantees 100 days of employment to all the eligible members of each family registered at the rate of Rs 258 (US$3.70) per day. The panchayat is expected to maintain a shelf of projects and employment is to be provided within 15 days after the person places a request. If the panchayat is not able to provide employment within 15 days of demanding the job, unemployment wages have to be provided. Panchayat will have to pay compensation for the delay of wages. Out of the total amount spent by the panchayat per year, 60 percent needs to be a labor component and this would be reimbursed by the central government. Out of the material cost, i.e., 40 percent of the total, three-fourths would be met by central government and one-fourth by state government. Although when the scheme was lodged, the idea was to spend the entire budget on soil and water conservation, land development, eco-restoration etc., in subsequent years, there was permission to include works related to asset formation as well.

about Rs 231 (US$3.35); whereas repair work would fetch them Rs 258 (US$3.70) per day. Very few women work in more than one home and earn more. Preference is for work available near their home. There is reason for the desire for engagement in DRR-generated employment, which in turn is for solving one of their perennial problems. Employment near home enables more participation in community activities.

At panchayat level, the situation has reached a sort of TINA point (There Is No Alternative) except going in for the non-rubble-mounted alternatives. The rubble-mounted wall work is undertaken by contractors who might collude with the engineers and profiteer compromising on the quality of work. Often local formal and informal leaders have to be pacified with money to prevent possible trouble-making by way of reporting to vigilance even in cases of honest work. The restrictions against quarrying, unavailability of granite rubbles, exhaustion of material of currently licensed quarries, the multilayered license procedures,[11] nokkukoolie[12] at the quarry and work sites, speed money to the police during transportation, lack of good roads to take the rubble to the work spot, denial of permission by private parties to drive through their compound to download the rubbles together make the rubble-mounted protection wall a very unattractive work for the contractor, especially when the work is small in magnitude and cannot contain the "unaccountable" expenses. If the money is not paid, the extorters can "scrupulously" inspect the rubbles and raise inconvenient questions about the conformity of the stipulated size of the rubbles[13] and land up the contractor in heavy loss and could even prevent the very execution of the work. Hence contractors are reluctant to take up small works such as repairing of a 100-m gap.

---

[11]Clearance is required through DEAC (District Expert Appraisal Committee) and DEIAA (District Level Environment Impact Assessment Authority) and if required to be taken up to SPEIA (State Environment Impact Assessment Committee).

[12]A phenomenon found particularly in the state of Kerala where the organized labor force extort labor charges even if they do not do any work in the location, in the eventuality of some other agency undertaking the work at the behest of the person who wants to get the work done for wages. The term gawking wages also is being used to denote the same.

[13]The stipulated size is 1m^3 (meter cubed) for regular rubbles and below I m^3 for irregular rubbles.

There are two Balasabhas[14] in Ward 18. The participation of children can be assured for keeping vigil to protect the public property and for reporting need for repairs. Thus children can experientially get trained on civic sense and responsible citizenship. Instances of drug abuse by children are being reported and in response, Excise Department is conducting awareness generation classes. Involvement in DRR activities can provide meaningful engagement for children and reduce the possibility of drug addiction. When women are organized around DRR activities, probably they could develop strength to resist such local-level goondaism.

The Choice of the Project

SWOT is a data capture tool. Final choice of the project can be made only after a detailed analysis based on financial, economic technical, political, social, ecological and implementation viabilities. But SWOT analysis definitely brings our Gj/cPW as the most effective project, which can solve the problems of women related to sea incursion under the constraints of decision-making at panchayat level. It makes the most vulnerable potential victims that is, women, active agents and drivers to prevent disasters. Once a robust engendered implementation mechanism is in place, the local women become the implementers of the preventive measures against a perennial problem, which had been plaguing them for the last 10 years. They can be legitimately expected to discharge the DRR work most devotedly, this work being a solution for their day-to-day problems.

Women, fetching income into the house through labor, can benefit through the higher status and gender role reversal within the home. They enjoy higher economic independence, increased freedom to make

---

[14]The Balasabhas are the network of children in a ward. Each Sabha consists of 15to 30 children in the age group of 6 to 18 years, constituted with the purpose of preventing the intergenerational poverty transmission and the intended route toward this is capability enhancement of children. Study groups are constituted for experimental and systematic learning, for understanding democratic process, participation in conserving environment etc. This helps children to understand the intricacies of collectivization. At present, 66,743 Balasabhas, covering 10,59,283 children, creating glorious dimensions to the endeavor. Balasabha is set as the three-tier system as NHG, ADS, and CDS level.

financial decisions, and enlarged entry into the public places and en-hanced sharing of sociopolitical power (Pankaj 2010 pp. 50–52).

Not only the women in the currently unutilized labor pool, but also the currently unemployed women outside the pool as well, get a chance for wage earning. An engendered implementation mechanism has the po-tential to make them supervisors, labor supervisors, and labor contractors. Opportunities open up for learning new skills - not only the direct con-struction skills, but also the skills for becoming more effective members in the community. They can also learn to become creators of a culture of responsible citizenship (by preserving the construction against van-dalism and theft and making their voices heard in appropriate forums). Once they are more immersed in the community affairs, lobbying and negotiating skills develop eventually and could even lead up to taking the matter to higher levels for the solution of more robust, durable and per-haps much more expensive protection walls which can offer a permanent solution.

All the above benefits accrue to the local women when the choice is made of Gj/cPW technology. Choosing this technology enhances the in-come of women and becomes instrumental in reducing the vulnerability of women. As discussed in the literature, vulnerability is not a function of income poverty alone. Lack of information and knowledge about DM and DRR, lack of participation in DRR, lack of access to networks, lack of capacity to prevent disasters, lack of voice in decision-making spaces, etc. contribute to vulnerability to disasters. As discussed, Gj/cPW tech-nology not only provides opportunity for income generation for women, but also eliminates or reduces the current and future intangible aspects of vulnerability. Hence Gj/cPW can be a preliminary choice from the point of view of these obvious criteria and also from the point of view of reduc-ing the vulnerability of women to disasters. Effective DRR contributes to development and participation of women and children lends sustain-ability to this development.

Conclusion

Since tackling issues related to rubble-mounted protection wall is beyond the jurisdiction of the panchayat, the temporary solution is sought and mainly the comparisons are made between GTPW and Gj/cPW. When the factors for reduction of vulnerability of women—lack of employment, low income, lesser opportunities for social action, lesser control over the raging sea—are considered, Gj/cPW opens up the possibilities for tackling all these. The issues were analyzed in the larger context of bureaucratic and ground-level unwelcome practices. Gj/cPW comes up as the most likely temporary solution for the problems of the citizens in general and women in particular. Gj/cPW offers labor participation, income for women, future and eventual possibilities of community participation and participation in local political affairs. Income generation elevates the status of women within and outside their homes. Immersion in the community affairs give them control and participation over larger forces, which makes decisions about, say the preventive measures against sea incursion. Thus, Gj/cPW carries the potential to reduce their vulnerabilities.

A SWOT analysis is only a data capture tool. But all data have to be captured and put on the table transparently for the decision-makers (in this case, panchayat samithy) to see and to initiate a fact-based and evidence-based discussion. Again, a SWOT not only facilitates the discussion of the current situation, but also forces thinking about future opportunities. Being a data capture tool alone, further exploration and rigorous analysis is required regarding various types of viabilities mentioned earlier. The contribution of this study is that the methodology of a SWOT analysis can be taught and applied for data capture in decision-making for project alternatives and such discussions by all stakeholders together around this framework can bring to table all the dimensions of the issue and lend transparency regarding decision-making criteria. Such discussions will bring to focus the larger systemic issues (for example those related to rubble-mounted sea wall) which, if handled at a higher level, can provide permanent solutions and prevent catastrophic damages in the case of a cataclysmic hazard. A SWOT analysis is used as a tool to engender DRR. Through SWOT, in discussions on DRR, the gender issues can be made visible and views can be generated to engender DRR initiatives. While technology is chosen for DRR, the technology needs to be assessed in terms of the reduction of vulnerability of women.

References

ACOG (American College of Obstetricians and Gynecologists). 2010. *Preparing for Disasters: Perspectives on Women.* https://www.acog.org/ Clinical-Guidance-and-Publications/Committee-Opinions/Committee-on-Health-Care-for-Underscored-Women/Preparing-for-Disasters-Perspectives-on-Women, (accessed June 21, 2018).

Anderson, M. B. 1994. "Understanding the Disaster-Development Continuum: Gender Analysis Is the Essential Tool." *Focus on Gender* 2, no. 1, pp. 7–10. Development Continuum: Gender Analysis Is the Essential Tool

Bradshaw, S., and M. Fordham. 2013. *Women, Girls and Disasters, A review for DFID.* London, UK: Middlesex University.

CP (Chellanam Panchayat). 2017. *625 Is the Number of Families Who Require Houses.* http://lsgkerala.in/chellanampanchayat/files/2017/06/ grama_sabha_list__2016.pdf

DCO (Directorate of Census Operations). 2011. *Census of India 2011: District Census Handbook Ernakulam.* Thiruvananthapuram, India: DCO.

Enarson, E. 2000. *Gender and Natural Disasters.* Geneva, Switzerland. InFocuProgramme on Crisis Response and Reconstruction. Working Paper 1, ISBN No. 92-2-112260-3. http://www.ilo.int/wcmsp5/groups/ public/---ed_emp/---emp_ent/---ifp_crisis/documents/publication/ wcms_116391.pdf

GOI (Government of India) Ministry of Home Affairs. 2009. *National Policy on Disaster Management.* New Delhi, India: GOI. https:// ndma.gov.in/images/guidelines/national-dm-policy2009.pdf

GOI (Government of India) National Disaster Management Authority. 2005. Disaster Management Act, December 23, 2005. https://ndma. gov.in/images/ndma-pdf/DM_act2005.pdf

Jawahar, M. n.d. *Report on Visit to Kudumbashree Institutions.* Thiruvananthapuram, India: Kudumbashree.

KS (Kudumbasree). 2017. *Balasabha.* http://www.kudumbashree.org/ pages/66#, (accessed August 26, 2017).

Morrison, M. 2012. *How Do I Do SWOT Analysis.* https://rapidbi.com/ how-do-i-do-a-swot-analysis

Morrison, M. 2016. *SWOT (TOWS matrix) Analysis Made Simple*. https://rapidbi.com/swotanalysis

Neumayer, E., and T. Plumper. 2007. "The Gendered Nature of Natural Disasters: The Impact of Catastrophic Events on the Gender Gap in Life Expectancy. 1981–2002." *Annals of the American Association of Geographers* 97, no. 3, pp. 551–66.

Pankaj, A. July 24, 2010. "Empowerment Effects of the NREGS on Women Worker: A Study in Four States." *EPW (Economic and Political Weekly)* 45, no. 30. http://www.environmentportal.in/files/Empowerment%20Effects%20of%20the%20NREGS.pdf

Sammut-Bonnici, T., and D. Galea. 2015 *SWOT Analysis*. Wiley Online Library. Wiley Encyclopedia on Management. https://doi.org/10.1002/9781118785317.weom120103

SOM (Steering Committee on Economic and Technical Cooperation) (SME), Policy Partnership on Women and Economy (PPWE). 2015. "Good Practices on Economic Empowerment of Women in Post-Disaster Reconstruction in Tohoku and the Asia-Pacific." Singapore: Asia-Pacific Economic Cooperation. APEC#215-ES-01.3.

Team FME. 2013. *SWOT Analysis: Strategy Skills*. Team FME. www.free-management-ebooks.com. ISBN 978-1-62620-951-0. http://www.free-management-ebooks.com/dldebk-pdf/fme-swot-analysis.pdf

Tozier, A, and B. Ange. 2015. "From Yokohama to Sendai: Approaches to Participation in International Disaster Risk Reduction Frameworks." *International Journal of Disaster Risk Science* 6, pp. 18–19. https://link.springer.com/article/10.1007/s13753-015-0053-6

Twigg, J. 2001. *Corporate Social Responsibility and disaster Reduction: A Global Overview*. London, UK: Overseas Development Institute.

UNDP (United Nations Development Programme). 2015. *Transforming Our World, the 2030 Agenda for Sustainable Development*. https://sustainabledevelopment. un.org/content/documents/21252030%20Agenda%20for%20Sustainable%20Development%20web.pdf

UNESC (United Nations Economic and Social Council) Commission on the Status of Women 2014. Report on the 58th session. "Gender Equality and Empowerment of Women in Natural Disasters." E/CN.6/2014/L.4. http://www.gender.go.jp/policy/saigai/pdf/58th_gender_equality_e.pdf

UNISDR (The United Nations Office for Disaster Risk Reduction). 2002. *ISDR Background paper for WSSD*. Geneva, Switzerland: UNISDR. http://gfmc.online/wp-content/uploads/ISDR-WSSD-Background-Paper-Version-June-2002-2.pdf

UNISDR (The United Nations Office for Disaster Risk Reduction). 2009. *UNISDR Terminology on Disaster Risk Rduction*. Geneva, Switzerland: UNISDR. https://www.unisdr.org/files/7817_UNISDRT erminologyEnglish.pdf

USAID (US Agency for International Development). 2011. "An Introduction to Disaster Risk Reduction" https://www.preventionweb.net/files/26081_kp1 concepdisasterrisk1.pdf

Wagner, D. 2016. "Learning, Literacy and Sustainable Development: Inclusion, Vulnerability and SDGs." In *Children and Sustainable Development Ecological Education in a Globalized World*, eds. A. Battro, P. Lena, M. S. Sorondo and V. J. Braun, (pp. 45–65). Philadelphia, PA: Springer. http://www.thecollo.org/gpsd/resources/WAGNER_Learn-Sustain_Vatican_dw_v3.1c_June2_16.pdf

Wisner, B. Blaike, P. Cannon, T. and Davis, I. 2003. *At Risk: Natural Hazards, People's Vulnerability and Disasters*. Abingdon, UK: Routledge. https://www.amazon.com/At-Risk-Vulnerability-Disasters-2003-12-21/dp/B01FKS90Y8

CHAPTER 6

Impact of Climate Change on Women's Health in Bangladesh

Mst Marzina Begum

Department of Public Administration, University of Rajshahi, Rajshahi, Bangladesh

Introduction

The total population of Bangladesh is approximately 161 million as of 2015 (Global Partnership 2016), and the United Nations Population Division (UNPD) projected that this would reach around 218 million by 2050 (Peter and Zunaid 2008). There is no doubt that the current population size itself is a burden given the geographical territory. No doubt that it is very hard to ensure a proper balance between the size of the population and actual requirement of health services. In 2015, the Bureau of Statistics (BBS) of the Government of Bangladesh (GoB) pointed out that the country was still considered as a rural-based country, since more than 70 percent of the total population lived in rural areas, which were not adequately covered with proper health services. Though the extent of poverty has been reduced from 57 percent in 1991 to 24.7 percent in 2015 (Ahmed et al. 2015), poor health care facilities still remain, particularly in rural areas. In 24 percent of urban people are also not served well in basic health necessities including sanitation and portable water (Islam and Biswas 2014).

Climate changes very rapidly at both the national and global levels. Given the context, the Intergovernmental Panel on Climate Change

(IPCC) in its third assessment report predicts climate change as likely to be compounded by poor human health (McCarthy et al. 2001). People of Bangladesh suffer from poor health due to extreme natural events including floods, storms, droughts, and heat waves. Alarmingly, it is projected that the worst impact of climate change on health will have future consequences for most of the population in Bangladesh. Climate change brings new and emerging health complexities and women are especially affected. The vulnerabilities caused by climate change may put the health and very lives of women at risk. This chapter examines the impacts of climate change on the health risks and vulnerabilities of Bangladeshi women.

Climate Change and Health

The IPCC refers to climate change as any change in climate that occurs over a period of time, due to natural variability or human actions (McCarthy et al. 2001). Climate changes are always varied due to natural phenomena; on the other hand, human activities also contribute to global climate change. For example, increased global temperatures and extreme heat waves are associated with burning of fossil fuels. Considering the role of human activities in climatic change, United Nations Framework Convention on Climate Change (UNFCCC 1992, Article, 1) finds climate change directly or indirectly due to human activities is responsible for change in the global environment.

However, the meaning of health is explained as "a state of complete physical, mental and social well-being and merely not an absence of disease or infirmity" (Ministry of Health and Family Welfare [MoHFW] 2008, p.1). There is no doubt that sustainable development starts with a safe and healthy life (Nanan and White 2014). Therefore, Sustainable Development Goal (SDGs) 3 focuses on better health care and well-being for all ages and is at the forefront of the agenda of the UN goals. However, health is not only a subject of biology, but also a societal architecture that requires human intervention (World Health Organization [WHO] 2008a).

Health and well-being is a primary indicator to the improved quality of life. Highlighting the importance of health care system, the international declaration of health rights adopted by the WHO says in its preamble that "the enjoyment of the highest attainable standard of health is one of the fundamental rights of every human being." While defining women's physical and mental health; women's well-being will be measured considering the social, political, economic, and biological context of their daily lives. On a particular note, when it comes to global health status of women, it is found that 43 percent of all women suffer from iron-deficiency anemia, and for pregnant women it is 56 percent (on average). It should be noted that in every year, about 10 million women suffer from health complexities and even death in the pregnancy period. Even if they are survived, this may sometimes lead to long-term physical and mental disability (Paul et al. 2014).

Nexus between Climate Change and Human Health

During COP 21 (Paris) summit various news media reported that Bangladesh ranks as the sixth riskiest zone due to climate change. In order to meet the future challenges, the GoB established the "Climate Change and Health Promotion Unit." The terms of reference of the unit include promoting health services to fight against the negative effects of climate change. The unit is also responsible for ensuring healthy lives for the residents, and projecting health risks and vulnerabilities in the country.

However, climate change poses a wide range of risks and vulnerabilities to human health in the twenty-first century and have been analyzed both environmentally and economically. IPCC (2014) acknowledges that health risks and vulnerabilities between men and women due to climate change are varied on a number of levels, due to different economic, social, and psychological factors. Bangladesh achieved some parts of the targets of the Millennium Development Goals (MDGs), and progressed in reducing maternal death, but still there are huge challenges in the health sector. On the other side, Sustainable Development Goals (SDGs) 3, 6 and 11 by the UN directly focus on health issues and well-being. Over the last two decades, Bangladesh has achieved success in human development index (for example, sustained increases in the life expectancy rates, and reduction of child and maternal mortalities). However, changing climatic conditions are expected to hamper achieving the desired quality of health for people as changing climatic conditions increases the number of illnesses and deaths. These are regarded as weather-related morbidity and mortality (Muthukumara 2014). Hence, extreme climate events drive many of the health-related problems of women.

WHO focused on three key messages in a report entitled "Climate Change and Health Impacts: How Vulnerable Is Bangladesh and What Needs to Be Done" (Muthukumara 2014).This report points out that climate change will have a serious consequence on health by 2050. The report also says that the consequences of environmental migration contribute to the growing urban slum that is rapidly changing population dynamics. This environment-generated migration has considerable adverse consequences for climate-induced health risks and vulnerabilities in the urban areas in Bangladesh. The report continued to argue that in a cost-effective way, health services should be provided. A cost-effective approach in the health sector can reduce the burden of vulnerable and poorer groups of the population. In the process, the country must deal with effective budgetary allocation to ensure better health support for the most vulnerable people who have a low capacity to adapt to the health complications arising out of climate change.

People are exposed directly to changing climate, such as increases in temperature and rainfall events, changes in precipitation pattern, and rising sea-level. It is noted that agricultural production is directly linked to the patterns of precipitation, and this impacts on food security and nutritional status of the population. However, medical sciences have already proven that continuous intake of low calories result in a form of malnutrition, particularly in women and young children of reproductive age. On the other hand, climate change has also been one of the main causes to land degradation, decline of freshwater and coastal ecosystems, destruction of biodiversity, and stratospheric ozone depletion; hence, these issues have a large impact on health (Rahman 2008).

About 8.3 million people in Bangladesh are now living in cyclone-prone areas in Bangladesh and that is expected to increase to 20.3 million by 2050 (WHO 2015). Climate change is felt at a deeper level by the vulnerable people, who have the low resources and capacities to deal with the hazard. More interestingly, research has shown that women and young girls have very low level of knowledge on disaster preparedness and organizing for recovery. As a result, women suffer to higher death rates than male after a disaster. For instance, the cyclone of 1991 in Bangladesh showed that among the reported 140,000 dead or missing, 90 percent were found to be women (Kamal and Umama 2015). An important study on sexual harassment, carried out by Nasreen (2012), showed that 71.6 percent of women were victims of sexual harassment during disasters, and women and young girls faced with increased physical and psychological violence. Nasreen (2012) also reported that some women and girls faced sexual harassment even in cyclone shelters. So, state machineries have failed to provide personal safety and security of women during disasters. These conditions become worse, if women and young girls had any form of physical and mental disability (Nasreen 2012). On the other hand, it was highlighted that due to changes in climate, men are usually concerned about the irrigation process and agriculture production, while women are worried about their health rights issues (Sachi 2015).

Temperature and Extreme Weather

According to the Global Climate Risk Ranking, Bangladesh had 4,729 deaths due to extreme climatic conditions from 1994 to 2013 (Kreft et al. 2015). Bangladesh Centre for Advanced Studies (BCAS) and the National Institute of Preventive and Social Medicine (NIPSOM), in a joint study, point out that temperature (maximum and minimum), rainfall (annual and seasonal), and salinity in water and soil caused the occurrence of several weather-related infectious diseases. There are yearly records on temperature conducted and maintained by public agencies and researchers as well in Bangladesh that present extreme heat waves (Ministry of Environment and Forest 2009). On the other hand, there are some health-related complications connected with heat illness, for instance, heat exhaustion, dehydration, respiratory and cardiovascular-related diseases in elderly people (Rahman 2008). So, the country is particularly susceptible to heat waves.

In 2008, WHO (2008b) estimated that heat wave and extreme temperatures increase vector-borne diseases, such as the transmission of malaria in some locations. Heat waves are responsible for killing approximately one million people every year in the world. When it comes to the case of Bangladesh, having visited the MoHFW website, it does not provide specific data on illnesses and deaths due to extreme heat waves. But, without providing any data, the MoHFW claims some progress toward the elimination of vector-borne diseases has recently been made. Pregnant women and young girls are still exposed to malaria, as mosquitoes are the main transmitter of malaria mostly found around household areas, where, on an average, women spend 66 percent of their daily time at home, compared to men who spend on an average 45 percent of their daily time at home (The Daily Star 2016). Malaria in pregnant women is associated with the risk of miscarriage, premature delivery, increased risk of low weight at birth, and other adverse health consequences. Rahman (2008) in a study on women affected by malaria found that the abdomen of women during pregnancy is more likely on average 0.7°C warmer, compared to nonpregnant women.

It is also observed that diarrhea diseases increased whenever there was an increase in temperature and heat waves (Rahman 2008). Diarrhea remains leading infectious cause of death in Bangladesh. In May 2014, WHO published a report stating that diarrhea-related deaths in Bangladesh reached 15,928, which is 2.19 percent of the total deaths of the country (Rahman 2008).

Some earlier studies explored the nexus between excess temperature and the extent of eclampsia during pregnancy. Increased hypertension is linked with greater occurrence with the pregnant women who are staying in the coastal areas, when temperature is high. Research showed that the hypertension rates related to pregnancy was the highest in June, since at that time the level of temperature was very high, and the humidity level gets at its lowest point. There are well-established research findings that an extreme heat wave poses serious health risks, causing many deaths in each year. There is also a likelihood that a 2°C increase in temperature would amplify the death rates in the world. However, it is reported that direct exposure to heat could kill as many as 60,000 people in Bangladesh in the coming years ahead (Rahman 2008).

Waterlogging and Saline Contamination

In the southwestern part of Bangladesh, waterlogging has emerged as a big challenge for women's health. Women are often more severely affected than men in their multiple roles of agriculture as producers of food and primary household providers to maintain health and well-being of other members of family. Women are the first responder in each family who do all sorts of water security for their family members and for livestock. Hence, women need to spend much time in waterlogged premises. Women are forced to drink water that is not safe, as many of the tube wells get contaminated in different settings, which poses serious health risks. It has been found that there are increased rates of gynecology-related health complexities due to the use and drinking of polluted water. Pregnant women also have difficulties with mobility in slippery conditions and waterlogging. Therefore, effects of climate change are varied between males and females in Bangladesh.

The coastal region has 19 districts, which cover 32 percent of the total area of Bangladesh, and more than 35 million people live there (Mahmuduzzaman et al. 2014). However, there is increased salinization of water and soil and the coastal people suffer heavily from the lack of water for safe drinking water, agricultural production, and other household purposes. Apart from that, the ecological environment of the coastal region is affected by salinity, as it has negative effects on agricultural production, water quality, and terrestrial biodiversity. However, a study showed that the salinization of fresh water is continuing to increase, for instance, in 1973 it was 8,330km^2 but increased to 10,560km^2 in 2009 (SRDI 2010).

As stated, salinity intrusion in drinking water has direct adverse impacts on health. In the coastal areas, the sources of natural drinking water (including rivers and groundwater) in the coastal areas are affected by saltwater intrusion from the sea. Furthermore, groundwater, soils, and many rivers are threatened due to salinization arising from tidal waves and heavy storms (Rony et al. 2016). On a particular note, salinity intrusion is projected to get worse in the future due to sea-level rise (WHO 2008b). A report on salinization of fresh water carried out by the WHO that more than 7.6 million additional people could be affected by the "very high salinity" (>5 parts per thousand) by 2050 in coastal areas (WHO 2015). Approximately 20 million people in Bangladesh are prone to climate risks due to the higher level of salinity as they highly depend on the flow of water from rivers, tube wells, and ponds for their daily washing, taking shower, and drinking water (Rony et al. 2016).

Sodium helps keep the body at a normal water balance. On the other side, if people overconsume the level of dietary intake of sodium, there will be negative consequences on their health, such as high blood pressure, brain problems, kidney problems, and other health complications (Rony et al. 2016). Throughout pregnancy physiological adaptation of women is very significant, where any variations from fetal to neonatal can be fatal to their life. Normally, hypertension (both diastolic and systolic blood pressures) is diagnosed in most cases after the 36th week of pregnancy (Rony et al. 2016). Pregnant women in coastal areas depend highly on the saline water for drinking. In that case, there is the presence of higher sodium level found in urine, and increased blood pressure.

Research by Rony et al. (2016) was undertaken to examine the impact of saline water intake on the health status of pregnant women in the two districts at Barguna and Patuakhaliin, Bangladesh. The extent of sodium (Na) in their urine was examined, and their blood pressure was also measured. The diagnostic report presented that sodium (Na) level, and blood pressure (BP) during the pregnancy was the highest in the 2nd trimester followed by the 3rd trimester and the 1st trimester (Rony et al. 2016). Just to say that a trimester means a period of 3 months in case of pregnancy, as normal pregnancy is divided into three trimesters.

As stated, the salinization of water and soil are projected to further deteriorate through future changes in climatic conditions, more specifically due to sea-level rises. Khan et al. (2011) conducted research and found that there are higher incidents of gestational hypertension diagnosed in pregnant women who lived in the southwestern coastal area that lead to preeclampsia, compared to those living in other areas. Local doctors and community representatives have blamed the excess salinized content in the drinking water. To them, this condition exposes risks to women in the coastal areas that may result in excess maternal mortality and morbidity (Khan et al. 2011).

Drought and Arsenic Poisoning

Drought is a form of natural disaster that leads to food insecurity and many health complications that can damage livelihood patterns of people. Women and young girls hold water pots and buckets or narrow-mouthed big containers that are placed on top of their head and carried until home. During the emergency period of drought, women have to make a long journey in order to reach the nearest tube wells and then bring back the weighty water pots, which causes fatigue and early damage to bones. However, in the northwestern region of Bangladesh, during the dry season, women and young children may have to go out to find out their sources of water for at least two times each day depending on the water requirement of their family members. Added to that, the first trip often takes place before the sunrise, which minimizes the required amount of sleeping; these skipped hours of sleep pose terrible side effects on women's mind and body in the long run. It is revealed that during the dry season in rural Bangladesh, a significant percentage of women's daily lives involved collecting water for their families and livestock. Furthermore, carrying heavy loads on head or waist for a long time causes huge damage to the cervical cord, the back muscles; and this can weaken and accelerate premature ageing of women.

Arsenic contamination was first detected in 1993 in Bangladesh (UNICEF 2008). The maximum level of acceptable level of arsenic contamination in water is 50 ppb (parts per billion). Tube wells are the dominant source of drinking water in the drought-prone areas of Bangladesh, but tube wells are highly exposed to arsenic contamination (WHO 2008b). Bangladesh Atomic Energy Commission finds that the concentration ranges between 150 and 200 ppb in most of the tube-well water in the different administrative districts near West Bengal of India, and almost 80 million people of the country who depend on tube well are exposed to arsenic who have the possibility of getting cancer in the future from arsenic poisoning (Uddin et al. 2004). There are 8.6 million tube wells in Bangladesh, among them 4.75 million (55 percent) were measured to test the level of concentration of arsenic. The experiment showed that 3.3 million (39 percent) were identified as green without contamination, and these tube wells are considered as a safe source of drinking water (UNICEF 2008). On the other hand, 1.4 million (16 percent) were identified in the "red" category, meaning these are not safe for use as drinking water source due to a high arsenic level (UNICEF 2008). However, medical science has already proven that health complexities due to arsenic contamination cause skin lesions, kidney and liver problems, swelling of the affected areas, and numbness in the hands and legs (WHO 2018).

Water and Vector-Borne Disease

Having reviewed the data on flood, every year Bangladesh faces flood risks due to climate change. It is estimated that by 2030, 4.2 million people would be exposed at higher risks due to river floods annually (WHO 2015). No doubt, flooding causes difficulties to the livelihood of people in the affected areas. McCarthy et al. (2001) point out that flooding causes an increase in the occurrence of vector-borne and water-borne diseases. Given the scenario, it means that Bangladesh is vulnerable to outbreaks of infectious diseases including water-borne diseases (e.g., diarrhea, dysentery), and vector-borne diseases (e.g., malaria, dengue, etc.). According to data retrieved from the disease control cell of the Health Department of the GoB, from January 1 to November 30, 2016, a total of 5,823 people were diagnosed and admitted to the different hospitals with dengue fever. Global data shows that one-third of the world's population lives in areas where dengue transmission is very high (Rahman 2008). Therefore, more actions are required to uncover health complications related to water-borne, water-washed, and water-related ailments.

On the other hand, WHO says that malaria is the deadliest vector-borne disease. To them, malaria is responsible for an estimated 660,000 deaths in the single year 2010 worldwide and most of the deaths were of African children. However, dengue has become one of the world's fastest growing vector-borne diseases, which has seen a30-fold increase over the last 50 years. The Institute of Epidemiology Disease Control and Research (IEDCR), and the Centre for Communicable Diseases conducted an empirical study (Jabbar 2014) from 2008 to 2009. They took samples of different medical college hospitals to measure the magnitude of dengue and malaria in six districts in Bangladesh. The study team found that dengue transmission was equally present in the urban (51 percent) and rural areas (49 percent), and it is common throughout the year but most commonly occurred (19 percent) during the post-monsoon period (September and October) (Jabbar 2014).

Long-standing values and norms of society and the poor attitude toward women makes them vulnerable during any climatic disaster. Apart from that, loss of privacy in cyclone shelters, and physical assault during the relief, simply discourage women to go to the designated location even during an emergency. Even after disasters, women are not allowed to go the community health care center alone, and they must be accompanied by their male counterparts.

Climate Change: Dealing with Women's Health in Bangladesh

McCarthy et al. (2001) refer to adaptive capacity in the form of human abilities to deal with ensuing climate change and its consequences. However, the adaptive capacity remains inherent in the system that requires the resources and strategies in order to use it effectively for the purpose of adaptation. At the global level, in order to properly address climate change, there are some guidelines maintained by the UNFCCC. According to Article 4 of the UNFCCC, when proposing any new adaptation strategies, every country must evaluate the impact on people's health considered together with other environmental and economic factors and issues. When it comes to developing impact assessments, it fully recognizes the well-being of people with regard to health, and other related issues. The UNFCCC as a mission is to deal with the "adverse effects" of climate change; more importantly, it highlights its impact on "natural and managed ecosystems or on the operation of socio-economic systems" and also focuses on "human health and welfare" (UNFCCC 1992).

To lessen the impacts of climate change on human health, there are many approaches that range from infrastructure planning to a more development-oriented transformation. No doubt that any approaches must address the issues and build broader resilience to climate change. The question is how successful will Bangladesh be in coping with the climate change challenges to women's health? To deal with these crises, the GoB has already taken some major steps to address climate change risks and vulnerabilities. In responding to the question, the National Health Policy in Bangladesh, introduced in 2011, mentioned some limited progress in climate change about salinized water and soil, drought, and emergency response through better preparedness system. Furthermore, the National Health Policy claims some achievement for eradication of some respiratory diseases, heat- and cold-wave-related health complications, water-borne and parasite-related problems such as malaria and dengue, and malnutrition (MoHFW 2011).

The GoB through the "Sixth Five Year (FY 2011-2015) Plan" recognized the future health risks due to climate change. The plan focused on "build(ing) capacity in the area of environmental health through both public and private sectors" (Planning Commission 2011). On the other side, in the Seventh Five Year Plan (FY 2015-2020), it has specific programs to implement the "Gender Action Plan on Climate Change (CCGAP)". There is no denying the fact that the impact of climatic changes on women's health differs due to the varying possession of individuals' access to resources, and the ability to make their own decisions that can help to build a climate-resilient society.

In order to deal with the future challenges of climate change, governments, partner countries, and international organizations plan to include women in their climate change adaptation programs at the community level. It is suggested that all programs regarding climate change are required to identify and reduce gender-based inequalities. Recently, the Ministry of Women and Children Affairs (MOWCA), Bangladesh Climate Change Trust Fund (BCCTF), and various nongovernment organizations have started to integrate gender sensitivity in their respective project design and monitoring aspects in climate adaptation programs.

The GoB introduced a *National Climate Change Fund*, which focused on climate change adaptation strategies. Apart from that, health has been included in the climate change strategy and action plan that was introduced in 2009. Again, it should be noted that there is the 10years' perspective plan for health for the period of 2010 to 2021 in regard to climate change (General Economic Division 2011). However, it is expected that a significant amount of the climate fund must go into adaptation programs in order to lessen negative impacts on women's health arising from climate change. This is argued to focus on the potential of women's capability and their initiatives to address risks and vulnerabilities. No doubt that women can be powerful agents whose indigenous knowledge will be helpful in coping with changing climate conditions, but the role of women is undervalued in the society of Bangladesh. It has been found that the potential responsibilities of women to respond to the changing climatic conditions, and resilience building, are generally underutilized at family, and community levels. Hence, women are needed to be fully incorporated into different climate change adaptation strategies and programs.

FAO (2009) revealed that women lack access to climate-related information and the shortage of information is a great obstacle for early preparation for their health issues and beyond. The IPCC explains that future healthcare must relate to climate change, because of the fact that sound physical health of population helps to sustain an adaptive capacity (Rahman 2008). From the findings, it can be said that in the changing climate change scenario, the health status of women is still far from the standard level, and women have very few roles to know risks and vulnerabilities.

Conclusion

From the above discussion, it is clear that Bangladesh now faces some challenges due to the impact of climate change, particularly for women's health. The government should introduce extreme-weather-tolerant efficient health services for all and develop a dataset for climate-related health complications, particularly for women. Undoubtedly, if strategies to deal with climate change are not efficient, then certainly climate-related infectious diseases could become more prominent, and bring new health risks and vulnerabilities to women. In every particular stage of climate change, women and young girls face health complications. So, priority should be given to include them in the disaster risk management process in order to build their own resilience capacity. Last but not least, it is necessary to focus on the emergence of community participation in dealing with the continuously changing climate, which relates to women's health risks and vulnerabilities in Bangladesh.

References

Ahmed, A. U., S. Haq, M. Nasreen, and R. H. A. Wali. 2015. "Climate Change and Disaster Management." Final Report, Sectoral Inputs towards the Formulation of Seventh Five Year Plan (2016–2021).

FAO (Food and Agriculture Organization). 2009. "FAO Profile for Climate Change." Rome, Italy.

General Economic Division. 2011. "Outline Perspective Plan ofBangladesh2010-2021: Making Vision 2021: A Reality." Dhaka, Bangladesh: Planning Commission, Government of the People's Republic of Bangladesh.

Global Partnership. 2016. "*Monitoring Profile-October 2016 Bangladesh.*" http://effectivecooperation.org/wp-content/uploads/2016/10/Bangladesh_4.10.pdf

IPCC (Intergovernmental Panel on Climate Change). 2014. "Climate Change 2014 Impacts, Adaptation and Vulnerability." Top Level Findings From Working Group II AR 5 Summary for Policy Makers - Assessing and Managing The Risks of Climate Change" http://ipcc-wg2.gov/AR5/images/uploads/WGII-AR5_SPM_Top-Level_Findings.pdf

Islam, A., and T. Biswas. November 20, 2014. "Health System in Bangladesh: Challenges and Opportunities." *American Journal of Health Research, Science Publishing Group* 2, no. 6, pp. 366–74.

Jabbar, M. A. 2014. "Vector Borne Diseases: Small Bites Can Be a Big Threat." *The Daily Star*, April7, 2014.

Kamal, A. M., and U. Umama. 2015. "Women's Sexual and Reproductive Health Hazards during Floods." *Dhaka Tribune*, May 23, 2015.

Khan, A. E., A. Ireson, S. Kovtas, S. K. Mojumder, A. Khusru, A. Rahman, and P. Vineis. 2011. "Drinking Water Salinity and Maternal Health in Coastal Bangladesh: Implications of Climate Change." *Environmental Health Perspectives* 119, no. 9, pp. 1328–32.

Kreft, S., D. Eckstein, L. Junghans, C. Kerestan, and U. Hagen. 2015. "Who Suffers Most from Extreme Weather Events? Weather-related Loss Events in 2013 and 1994 to 2013." Global Climate Risk index, Briefing Paper, Germanwatch, 2015, Berlin.www.germanwatch.org/en/cri

Mahmuduzzaman, M., Z. U.Ahmed, Nuruzzaman, A. K. M.Nuruzzaman, and F. R. S. Ahmed.2014. "Causes of Salinity Intrusion in Coastal Belt of Bangladesh." *International Journal of Plant Research* 4, no. 4A, pp. 8–13.

McCarthy, J. J., F. Osvaldo, N. A. Canziani, D. J. Leary, K. Dokken, and S. White. 2001. *Climate Change 2001: Impacts, Adaptation and Vulnerability of Climate Change*. Cambridge, UK: Cambridge University Press. Contribution of Working Group II to the Third Assessment Report of the Intergovernmental Panel on Climate Change, Published for the Intergovernmental Panel on Climate Change, pp. 1–1042.

Ministry of Health and Family Welfare. 2008. "National Health Policy 2008". Dhaka, Bangladesh: Government of the People's Republic of Bangladesh, pp.1–18.

Ministry of Environment and Forest. June, 2009. "Climate Change and Health Impact in Bangladesh". Dhaka, Bangladesh: Climate Change Cell, Department of Environment, Ministry of Environment and Forest, Component 4b, CDMP, MOFDM.

Ministry of Health and Family Welfare. 2011. "National Health Policy 2011". Dhaka, Bangladesh: Government of the People's Republic of Bangladesh, pp. 1–10.

Muthukumara, M. 2014. "When Climate Becomes a Health Issue: How Vulnerable is Bangladesh?" World Bank report. http://reliefweb.int/report/bangladesh/when-climate-becomes-health-issue-how-vulnerable-bangladesh

Nanan, D. J., and F. White. 2014. "Disaster risk reduction and sustainable development." *Global Journal of Medicine and Public Health* 3, no. 6. http://www.gjmedph.com/uploads/E-Vo3No6.pdf

Nasreen, M. 2012. "Women and Girls: Vulnerable or Resilient?" Dhaka, Bangladesh: Institute of Disaster Management and Vulnerability Studies, Dhaka University, Bangladesh.

Paul A., M. Murshed, and S. Akther. 2014. "Women Health and Disease Pattern in the Rural Areas of Bangladesh: A Case Study on Haimchar Upazila under Chandpur District." *Journal of Asiatic Society of Bangladesh* 40, no. 1, pp. 27–37.

Peter, K. S., and A. K. Zunaid. 2008. "Population Challenges for Bangladesh in the Coming Decades." *Journal of Health, Population and Nutrition* 26, no. 3, pp. 261–72. Special Issue on Achieving the Millennium Development Goals in Bangladesh (SEPTEMBER 2008).

Planning Commission. 2011. "Accelerating Growth and Reducing Poverty, Part- 1: Strategic Direction and Policy Framework." Dhaka, Bangladesh: Sixth Five Year Plan (FY 2011-2015), Planning Commission, Ministry of Planning, Government of the People's Republic of Bangladesh.

Rahman, A. 2008. "Climate Change and Its Impact on Health in Bangladesh." *Regional Health Forum* 12, no. 1, pp.16–26.

Rony, Z. I., S. I. Khan, A. Asgar, and G. Kibria. 2016. "Effects of Saline Water on Health Status of Pregnant Women in Coastal Regions of Bangladesh." *Asian Journal of Medical and Biological Research* ` no. 1, pp. 55–61.

Sachi, S. M. July, 2015. "Environment: Gender and Climate Change Adaptation." *Dhaka Tribune*, July 23, 2015.

SRDI (Soil Resources Development Institute). 2010. "Saline Soils of Bangladesh." Dhaka, Bangladesh: SRDI, Ministry of Agriculture.

The Daily Star. 2016. "Mosquito-Borne Diseases: Women at Risk, More than Men." A English National Daily Newspaper, 30 November, 2016. https://www.thedailystar.net/backpage/mosquito-borne-diseases-women-risk-more-men-1311769

Uddin, S. J., J. A. Shilpi, G. M. Murshid, A. A. Rahman, M. M. Sarder, and M. Alam. 2004. "Determination of the Binding Site of Arsenic on Bovine Serum Albumin Using Warfarin (site-I Specific Probe) and Diazepam (site-II Specific Probe)." *Journal Biological Science* 4, no. 5, pp. 609–12.

UNFCCC (United Nations Framework Convention on Climate Change). 1992. Article 1, Climate Change Secretariat, Geneva. www.unfccc.int

UNICEF (United Nations Children's Fund). 2008. *Arsenic Mitigation in Bangladesh*. http://www.unicef.org/bangladesh/Arsenic.pdf

WHO (World Health Organization). 2008a. "Closing the Gap in a Generation: Health Equity through Action on the Social Determinants of Health." http://www.who.int/social_determinants/thecommission/finalreport/en

WHO (World Health Organization). 2008b. "Gender Climate Change and Health." World Health Organization.http://www.who.int/globalchange/GenderClimateChangeHealthfinal.pdf

WHO (World Health Organization). 2015. "Climate Health Country Profile-2015 (Bangladesh)." Geneva, Switzerland: WHO.

WHO (World Health Organizations). 2018. "Arsenic, Key Fact." http://www.who.int/en/news-room/fact-sheets/detail/arsenic

CHAPTER 7

Managing E-Waste in Reducing Vulnerability and Enhancing Resilience

The Case of Bangladesh

Nahian Nabila Hoque, Barrister-at-Law

Associate Barrister, Legal Counsel, Dhaka, Bangladesh

and

Lecturer (Part-time), British School of Law, Dhaka, Bangladesh

Introduction

E-waste includes all those electrical and electronics items that are unserviceable and/or discarded as waste and contains hazardous substances that can damage public health and the environment if not properly managed (Electronic Redux Corp 2011). Being the greatest user of e-goods, developed countries produce huge volume of e-waste. Taking the opportunity of fewer regulatory burdens, these developed counties are encouraged to export e-waste to the developing countries for economic benefits instead of going through the process of e-waste treatment (Geeraerts, Illes, and Schweizer 2015). E-goods are one of the primary drivers of economic growth and improvement of human living standards, but at the same time e-waste is also widely recognized as harmful for public health and the environment as it contains hazardous substances such as mercury, lead, cadmium, arsenic, beryllium, and brominated flame retardants, and it produces toxins such as halogenated dioxins and furans (Green Peace 2009). Although e-waste is hazardous, complex, expensive to treat, and promotes illegal trading, the fact is that e-waste is also considered as a vital source of resources and an income-generating opportunity.

E-waste out of electronics devices is primarily produced by developing countries for commercial and economic benefits and are often illegally exported to developing countries every year, frequently violating the international law (Green Peace 2015). About 67 percent of e-waste, either undeclared or gray market, are being dumped in landfills or illegally exported to developing countries (Bradley 2014). Like any other waste, e-waste is also unwanted to the holder and the holder always intends to get rid of it. The global quantity of e-waste in 2014 comprised of 1.0 metric ton lamps, 3.0 metric ton small IT goods, 6.3 metric ton screens and monitors, 7.0 metric ton temperature-controlling equipment, 11.8 metric ton large electronics equipment, and 12.8 metric ton small electronics equipment (Baldé et al. 2014). This sheer volume of e-waste is globally considered as hazardous and problematic to the environment and mankind. Thus, dealing with e-waste, is a major concern for policy makers at the national and international levels.

The objectives of this chapter are to: (i) have a general overview of e-waste that is considered globally hazardous and problem to mankind and the environment; (ii) identify the e-waste problems, and legal rules/policy level initiatives of matters involving overall e-waste management particularly in Bangladesh; and (iii) provide suggestions for handling and managing used e-goods to cope with the existing situation and future e-waste challenges. In order to meet the said objectives attempts have been made to describe the meaning, problem, global quantity of waste, impact of e-waste to mankind and the environment, and managing and handling the situation with legal rules, particularly in Bangladesh. Various, books, articles, journals, and court directives were used for collecting information, data related to e-waste transboundary movement, and treatment practices in line with e-waste laws/policies at national and global levels. The chapter has been finalized after careful analysis of the data collected from these various sources.

What Is E-Waste

Electronics waste (E-waste) is waste, but it is different from others due to its hazardous character. Any substance or object that can no longer be used for its original purpose, has become damaged or unsuitable for use, is left-over, unwanted, or a burden on its holder, has become contaminated with something that presents a risk and, has a low or negative economic value, and being burden on the producer is considered as waste. Few substances are always waste, for example, production residue and substances resulting from a production process that is not, as it is, sought for subsequent use.

E-waste arises out of "at the end of life" or any "discarded item" that has circuitry or electrical components with power or battery supply (EU Directive 2012). The European Union Commission Directive (2002/96/ EC) defines e-waste as waste of electrical or electronics equipment (EEE) including all components, subassemblies, and consumables that are part of the product at the time of discarding. EEEs convert to waste at the time and place when their structure and state are no more capable of providing desired performance or may not be functional due to damage or its technology/design may no longer be state of the art or trendy (Pongracz et al. 2008). In simple terms, e-waste is the electronics products that have (i) become really unserviceable, nonworking condition, obsolete and un-wanted by the user; (ii) reached the end of their useful life; (iii) lost their functional as well as face value; and (iv) discarded, at some time, by the owner or user.

E-waste contains precious metals such as copper, silver, gold, palladium, platinum etc. along with hazardous substance, which warrants re-covering for reuse or preparations for reuse following a proper treatment process without causing harm to the environment. However, e-waste generally contains the pollutants listed Table 7.1.

Global Scenario of E-Waste

This is the twenty-first century and the electronics industry is at its boom, meaning the society is more dependent on electronics than ever before. An average person per day spends 45 percent of their time in propagation

Table 7.1 EEE components and associated pollutants

Name of EEE components	Name of associated pollutants
a. Computers	Lead, Mercury, Cadmium and Beryllium
b. Batteries (disposable, rechargeable and lithium)	Cadmium, Cobalt, Lead, Lithium, Mercury, Nickel, Silver and Zinc
c. Mobile Phones	Lithium, Copper, Tin, Cobalt, Indium, Antimony, Silver, Gold and Palladium
d. Photocopiers	Mercury, Selenium
e. Circuit Boards	Silver, Lead, Copper, Cadmium, Brominated flame proofing agent, Polychlorinated Biphenyls and Arsenic
f. Light Emitting Diodes (LED)	Arsenic
g. Liquid Crystal Displays (LED)	Mercury
h. Cathode Ray Tubes (CRT)	Cadmium, Lead

Source: Tanskanen (2013).

of electronics (Thomas and Revoir 2010). Approximately, more than two billion electronics devices were sold worldwide in 2014, which by 2020 is likely to be more than 7 billion (Koepp 2016). The number of smartphone users around the globe was predicted to exceed over two billion in 2016, increasing by about 12.6 percent from 2015 (Emarketer 2014). The technological development has been growing at a lightning speed with diversity, as improved version and more user friendly EEE items replace the previous ones. Thus, very often many EEE devices become e-waste after short-term usage (Planet Green 2018). The UNU ADDRESS project documents narrated that e-waste volume reached 50 metric ton in 2017. The UN Environment Programme reported in May 2015 that up to 90 percent of the world's e-waste, worth nearly US$19 billion, are illegally traded or dumped annually.

This huge volume of e-waste (as seen in Table 7.2) requires global awareness regarding the consequence of its impact on the environment and hence, and proper treatment in a legal way to reclaim valuable materials and safe managing of toxic materials in order to protect lives, livelihoods, and the environment.

Table 7.2 Global quantity of generated e-waste

Year	E-waste generation (metric ton)	Population (Billion)	E-waste generation (kg/inh.)
2010	33.8	6.8	5.0
2011	35.8	6.9	5.2
2012	37.8	6.9	5.4
2013	39.8	7.0	5.7
2014	41.8	7.1	5.9
2015	43.8	7.2	6.1
2016	45.7	7.3	6.3
2017	47.8	7.4	6.5
2018 Projected	49.8	7.4	6.7

Source: Baldé et al. (2017).

Problems of E-Waste

Undoubtedly, development and use of e-goods is in the best interest of a higher standard of living and increased prosperity for the nations. At the same time, the development and usage procedures of e-goods have been creating wastes and environmental problems at different levels. E-waste contains toxic substances, thus its improper disposal harms both environment and inhabitants. Every year globally (mostly in developed countries) 60 percent of discarded e-devices, the main source of e-waste, end up in landfills and 40 percent are recycled. Yet, in the recycling process almost 30 percent e-material cannot be recovered. Under the said situation, some e-waste are exported to developing countries where it is burnt for scrap that is a toxic job and hence it creates problems for living organisms and the environment (IFIXIT.ORG). E-waste is not only toxic but it has economic value and demand in the market, thus dealing with e-waste also creates problems at the level of management, trading, and policy implementation. However, this problem is seen as a statement; a condition to be improved; a difficulty to be eliminated and/or a question proposed for solution or consideration. Being able to solve problems involve: (i) dealing with a logical approach or interpretation of the problem; (ii) what rules/ways could be applied to solve the problems; and (iii) abstract brain-storming and creative solutions.

E-waste is relatively a new extension of a scenario in a world that is increasingly faster with growing development of technology (United Nations Sustainable Development Programme n.d). Hence, a major task/approach has come up to treat e-waste for reducing the concentration of hazardous chemicals and elements through recycling and/or recovery. The treatment process of e-waste warrants its handling, dumping, recycling, and trading; all these stages have practical problems that ultimately jeopardize human health and environment.

Handling of E-Waste

Handling is the primary/initial e-waste action that can be accomplished through either the traditional way or recycling. Scientifically controlled recycling has less risk but uncontrolled recycling is risky.

Dumping of E-Waste

Dumping is one of the most common methods of e-waste disposal. Being hazardous, e-waste pollutes air, water, soil, and it hurts the planet and all the habitants of it, living organisms including crops and non-crops. The dumping situation of e-waste in developing counties like Bangladesh is where it is at its worst (Ahamad 2017). The Environment and Social Development Organization (ESDO) study report states Bangladesh generated 2.8 million metric ton of e-wastes that were dumped in open land-fills, farmland, and in open sources of water bodies without considering/knowing the harmful effects.

E-Waste Recycling

During the recycling recovery process e-waste releases (i) original constituents of equipment such as lead and mercury; (ii) substances that are required to be included in the recovery processes, like cyanide; and (iii) substances that are formed by the recycling process, for example, dioxins. Improper recycling process in the informal sector of developing counties is a common scenario even though state-of-the-art facilities exist there. Due to recycling of e-waste, workers and local residents are exposed to toxic chemicals through inhalation, dust ingestion, dermal exposure, and oral intake. Inhalation and dust ingestion impose a range of potential occupational hazards including silicosis (Lepawsky and McNabb 2010). E-waste contains mercury, lead, and cadmium, which are recognized as source of health hazards (see Table 7.3).

Table 7.3 Impact of e-waste elements

Mercury	Lead	Cadmium
• Brain disorders • Kidney, renal and neurological damage • Leading to even death	• Learning disabilities • Mental retardation • Behavioral problems • Hearing impairment	• Lung damage • Fragility of bones • High blood pressure • Nerve &brain damage • Kidney & liver disease

Source: ESDO Report- 2010: Study on E-Waste: Bangladesh Situation.

E-waste constitutes a long-term effect involving vulnerable groups and generations to come. Informal sector e-waste activities are the source of environment-to-food-chain contamination, as contaminants may accumulate in agricultural land and be available for uptake by grazing livestock. In practice, processing e-waste generates the pollution present in environment (Liu et al. 2009). Common health problems are identified including diseases and problems related to skin, stomach, respiratory tract, and other organs (Tsydenova and Bengtsson 2011). However, the greatest danger is faced by workers involved in e-waste recycling process who suffer from tuberculosis, blood disease, anomalies in the immune system, lung cancer, and malfunctioning of kidney and respiratory system (*The Independent* 2018). Their future generations face birth defects, infant mortality, and underdevelopment of the brain in children (Prakash and Manhart 2010). Moreover, long–range transportation of pollutant has also been observed and atmospheric pollution exposure as well (Sepulveda et al. 2010).

Extracting valuable elements contained in e-waste, for example, copper and gold, etc. is a good source of income for a developing nation like Bangladesh (Aowsaf 2018). Nevertheless, the recycling sector of e-waste in Bangladesh is largely unregulated. The workers in the recycle sector are dominated by the urban poor with very low literacy levels and thus, have very little awareness of the potential hazards (Rashna and Naureen 2015). These e-waste workers are exposed to hazards leading to physical injuries and chronic ailments. A particular hazard for the workers is in the disassembly stage and mechanical treatment methods, which generate dusts from plastics, metals, ceramics, and silica (UNB Dhaka 2017). The dusts and the surrounding ambient air may pose inhalation hazards along with dermal exposure hazard to workers as well as the risk of environmental contamination (Tsydenova and Bengtsson 2011).

In Bangladesh mostly children are engaged in various e-waste recycling activities and they are more vulnerable to the hazards of e-waste. According to the ESDOs study, in Bangladesh about (i) 50,000 children are involved in the non-formal e-waste collection and recycle process; (ii) 15 percent child workers die during and after the work as an effect of e-waste recycling; and (iii) 83 percent people become sick and live with long-term illness. By its nature and due to various circumstances, working with e-waste recycling is likely to harm health, safety, and morale of children. Child workers are exposed to a variety of hazards, for example, falling objects, chemicals, abusive employers along with many other social problems related to human survival in such harsh environment; injuries and heavy metal exposure constitute two of the main threats for child workers (IPEC 2011).

The world seriously suffers from the e-waste problem and thus effective and efficient waste management policy and the application of regulatory controls are necessary to protect the environment (Pharino 2017). Proper e-waste management not only protects human health and the environment but also creates the opportunity to extract reusable precious metals such as copper, silver, gold, palladium, and platinum. The precious metal of e-waste is valuable in black market, which attracts illegal trading and organized crime groups (Hence, e-waste is an important global concern; every nation should (i) adapt regulations and restriction to address the EEE producers, consumers, and recyclers; (ii) outline laws and policies by different countries, similar in nature, as actions guide to reduce harm from the serious consequences of e-waste; and (iii) export e-waste keeping in view the global flows from the country of origin particularly to developing countries; and (iv) build capacity to manage e-waste better.

Legal Rules

The legal rules framework provides the relevant legislation, policy, and agreement under which e-waste are managed, regulated, and monitored. However, the legal rules framework for e-waste is composed of international and regional conventions such as The Basel Convention or EU Regulations respectively along with national legislations. The Basel Convention, 1989 attempts to: (i) reduce hazardous waste generation at source; (ii) promote and ensure environmental sound management (ESM) of hazardous waste; (iii) promote the proximity principle, advocating disposal as close to the source as possible; and (iv) regulate and monitor the remaining transboundary movements of hazardous waste. The Convention is not against hazardous waste trading but it imposes some trade restrictions on those hazardous materials that are deemed to require transboundary movement. For example, exporting waste should be of ESM capacity; and the shipment must go through prior informed consent (PIC) procedure. The Convention also allows parties to enter into bilateral, multilateral, or regional agreement on transboundary movements of hazardous waste.

With an intention to prevent and reduce adverse impacts on the environment and human health, the EU has introduced WEEE Directive (2002/96/EC) that came into force in 2003 to cover a wide range of issues to manage EEE waste. The directive includes (i) prevention of e-waste generation and promotion of reuse, recycling, and any other form of recovery of waste to reduce disposal; (ii) promotion of green design and production of electronics products based on the principle of producers' responsibility; (iii) making the producer responsible for financing turn-back and management of e-waste; and (iv) creating pressure for the global electrical and electronics industries to adopt EPR policies (Huisman 2012).

Bangladesh is a developing country with increasing usage of modern technology. The ESDO reported that, in 2010 the yearly consumption of electronics products in Bangladesh was 3.2 million and the country generated roughly 2.8 million metric ton of e-waste. However, safe disposal of huge e-wastes was not being followed strictly, unknowingly the harmful e-waste had been dumped in open landfills, farmland, and open water bodies (ESDO 2010). Bangladesh is one of the signatories of the

Basel Convention, ratified in 1993. According to the Import Policy Order, importing used EE goods are prohibited in Bangladesh; however, in reality huge quantities of e-waste exist in the informal sector of Bangladesh (Rashna and Naureen 2015). EEE goods recycling and dismantling is a growing business in Bangladesh but an e-waste dismantling facility is not available in the formal sector. E-waste recycling is being carried out in the informal sector where about 120,000 urban poor are involved in the recycling trade chain in Dhaka, Bangladesh (ESDO 2010). There are no specific guidelines or regulations on the recycling process of e-waste in Bangladesh. Presently, the country's e-waste/hazardous waste activities including production, import/export, and recycling etc. are being carried out under the provision of (i) *Bangladesh Environment Conservation Act 2010*; (ii) Chemical Substance Depleting Ozone Layer (Control) Policy 2004; (iii) Sound Pollution Policy 2006; (iv) Bangladesh Environment Conservation Policy 2010; (v) Hazardous Waste and Ship Breaking Waste Management Policy 2011; (vi) Bangladesh Bio-safety Rules 2012; (vii) Import Policy Order; (viii) National Environment Policy 1992; (ix) The Environmental Conservation Rules 1997; and (x) *The Environmental Court Act 2000*.

The Government of Bangladesh is in the process of adopting (i) the E-waste (Management and Handling) Rules, which is applicable to producers, dealers, collection centers, refurbishers, dismantlers, recyclers, auctioneers, consumers involved in manufacture, sale, purchase and processing electrical and electronics equipment or components; and defining their responsibilities; (ii) description of the grant of authorization, power to suspend or cancel an authorization; (iii) procedure for registration, environmental clearance, and renewal; (iv) procedure for transportation and storage of e-waste; (v) accident reports and follow-up; and (vi) segregation, dismantling, recycling, and disposal of e-waste (The Daily Observer 2017). The Department of Environment has already sent the E-waste Rules to the Ministry of Environment and Forests for feedback (Sheikh 2017).

Recommendations

Managing e-waste is a complex, multifaceted challenge that is associated with recycling systems and global aspects of illegal e-waste export. Due to the expansion in illegal exports, measures for controlling, dealing, and combating through international, regional, and national regulations, rules and legislative approach are required. Enforcing regulations for handling and illegal exporting may be considered to resolve the global challenge and it cannot be a single country's task. However, the suggestions below are focused on a developing country like Bangladesh:

A) The formal sector produces lower impacts and have better e-waste recycling efficiency in comparison to the informal sector. So, the prevalence of formal facilities in e-waste recycling sector needs to be ensured and strengthened.

B) To upgrade recycling capacity and practices, the informal recyclers may be organized into small enterprises matched with a legal framework and structure with a proper monitoring system.

C) Informal sector has limited access to financial resources. Thus, financial incentives may be provided to informal sector to formalize recycling. As mentioned, the informal sector does a huge amount of e-waste recycling but they do not have the resources to uptake proper precautions as (recycling following safety measures can be expensive). Thus, financing them can be a great initiative toward safe recycling.

D) To improve the e-waste recycling practices, incentive packages may be offered to those who comply with and care for environmental and health norms.

E) Informal recycling enables huge hazardous employment of vulnerable people and poor children with virtually no education and little awareness of the effects of e-waste processing. Awareness-raising programs and actions/activities should be considered and taken to protect their right against hazards.

F) A system is required so that producers take responsibility to reduce and eliminate hazardous substances from their products, thus produce long-lasting products that are simple to recycle.

G) Policy effort may be initiated to manage end of life of EE products focusing on mandating recycling systems, limiting the toxic content of products and seeking to control or ban illegal trading.

H) Civil Society of the country may promote green consumerism, community awareness on household waste segregation and its contribution to resource efficiency/knowledge dissemination.

I) Lack of adequate legislation, insufficient enforcement, and illegal activities are the common problems of the country that cannot be solved through mere precautions, thus formal financial incentives and proper regulations may be designed.

J) With lessons learned from the implementation of the EU Directive, Bangladesh may plan to develop regulations for handling e-waste, ensure proper monitoring of the e-waste activities, and regulate importing of e-waste.

K) Research system may be framed and undertaken to extrapolate suitable modern technology for managing, handling, and controlling e-waste and to identify adaptation constraints and their solutions.

Conclusion

The production and use of electronics objects are globally escalating and many contain hazardous materials and substances. E-waste needs proper handling and management and development of end-of-life treatment options. There is absence of organized e-wastes recycling facilities in Bangladesh and the entire system is informal and unorganized. On the other hand, in the name of technology up-gradation and to give people access to the awesome benefits of technology, the action of shifting burden of e-waste on developing nations like Bangladesh is a clever step by some developed nations for their own economic benefit. However, the enforcement of e-waste regulations are hindered by the economic incentives and will continue to be hindered due to lack of proper financial support of the formal sectors. This may encourage noncompliance, favouring the illegal markets and informal sectors.

Transboundary movement, that is, illegal export and access of e-waste in Bangladesh, is a common phenomenon of developed countries. To continue imposing restrictions will not be a wise decision for a country like Bangladesh, rather it will be difficult and costly to implement. Nevertheless, this might destroy the potential source of cost-effective raw materials that are needed for the development of society and employment and income opportunity of the vulnerable poor who depend on the e-waste-related activities for their livelihood. The matter is sensitive, very careful handling is required to address the e-waste problem, which poses threat to both human life and the environment. However, the environmental degradation and hazards for the living organisms has no national boundary and does not follow the policy division of nations. Therefore, nations, irrespective of their developed or developing status, need to work on a common platform to identify the e-waste problem with solutions, enact and adapt fair policy regulation dedicated to e-waste to keep the global environment safe for the inhabitants.

References

Ahamad, R. 2017. "E-Wastes, A Threat to Public Health." *Tritiyo Matra*. mhttp://www.newagebd.net/article/25979/e-wastes-a-threat-to-public-health

Aowsaf, S. M. A. 2018. "Treasure from Trash: E-Waste Recycling in Bangladesh." *Dhaka Tribune*. https://www.dhakatribune.com/opinion/special/2018/02/15/treasure-trash-e-waste-recycling-bangladesh

Baldé, C. P., V. Forti, V. Gray., R. Kuehr., and P. Stegmann. 2017. *The Global E-Waste Monitor – 2017*. Bonn/Geneva/Vienna: United Nations University (UNU), International Telecommunication Union (ITU) & International Solid Waste Association (ISWA) a.

Baldé, K., F. Wang, J. Huisman, and R. Kuehr. 2014. *The Global E-Waste Monitor-2014: Quantities, Flows and Resources*. Bonn, Germany: UNU-IAS.

Borthakur, A., and P. Singh. 2012. "Electronic Waste in India: Problems and Policies." *International Journal of Environmental Sciences* 3, no. 1, pp. 353–62.

Bradford, G. 1990. "Environmental Regulation in Europe: Hazardous Waste and Contaminated Sites." *North Western Journal of International Law & Business* 10, no. 3, pp. 397–441.

Bradley, L. 2014. "E-Waste in Developing Countries Endangers Environment, Locals." *USNEws & World Report L.P.*, August 1, 2014.

Electronic Redux Corp. 2011. "What Is E-Waste?" *Electronic Redux Corp*. http://www.bostonelectronicwaste.com

Emarketer. 2014. "2 Billion Consumers Worldwide to Get Smart (phones) by 2016." *emarketer*. http://www.emarketer.com/Article/2-Billion-Consumers-Worldwide-Smartphones-by-2016/1011694#sthash.0CGanVps.pdfxp1- *xp*dmm

ESDO. 2010. *Study on E-Waste: Bangladesh Situation, Environment and Social Development Organization-ESDO*. Dhaka, Bangladesh: ESDO.

Geeraerts, K., A. Illes, and J. P. Schweizer. 2015. *Illegal Shipment of E-Waste from the EU: A Case Study on Illegal E-Waste Export from the EU to China. A Study Compiled as Part of the EFFACE Project*. London, UK: IEEP.

Green Peace. 2009. *Oir Planet, Our Home*. Green Peace. https://www.green peace.org/publications/mixed-dioxins-furnas-background-2009.pdf

Green Peace. 2015. *Campaign Reports*. Green Peace. mwhttp://www .greenpeace.org/international/en/campaigns/detox/electronics/ the-e-waste-problem/where-does-e-waste-end-up

Huisman, J. 2012. "Eco-efficiency Evaluation of WEEE Take-back Systems." In *Waste Electrical and Electronic Equipment (WEEE) Herdbook*, eds. V. Goodship and A. Stevels, pp. 93–119. New York, NY: Elsevier Science.

International Programme on the Elimination of Child Labor (IPEC). 2011. *Children in Hazardous Work: What We Know, What We Need to Do*. Geneva, Switzerland: ILO. mhttp://www.ilo.org/ipecinfo/ product/viewProduct.do?productID=17035

Koepp, J. 2016. *End to End Tests Are Essential for Matching Application Behavior to Network If IoT Is to Succeed*. http://www.newelectronics.co.uk /electronics-technology/end-to-end-tests-are-essential-for-matching-application-behaviour-to-network-if-iot-is-to-succeed/114053

Lepawsky, J., and C. McNabb. 2010. "Mapping International Flows of Electronic Waste." *Canadian Geographer* 54, no. 2, pp. 177–95.

Liu, Q., J. Cao., K. Q. Li., X. H. Miao., G. Li., F. Y. Fan., and Y. C. ZhaoC. 2009. "Chromosomal Aberrations and DNA Damage in Human Populations Exposed to the Processing of Electronic Waste." *Environmental Science and Pollution Research* 16, no. 3, pp. 329–38.

Pharino, C. 2017. *Challenges for Sustainable Solid Waste Management: Lessons from Thailand*. Berlin, Germany: Springer.

Planet Green. 2018. "E-Waste Crisis." *Planet Green*. mhttp://planetgreen recycle.com/fundraising/e-waste-problem

Pongracz, E., J. Yla-Mella., P. Tanskanen, and R. L. Keiski, L. 2008. "Proceedings of the 23rd International Conference on Solid Waste

Technology and Management." *Journal of Solid Waste Technology and Management* 16, no. Chapter 3-C, p. 18. Philadelphia, PA; March 30-April 2, 2008.

Prakash, S., and A. Manhart. 2010. *Socio-economic Assessment and Feasibility Study on Sustainable E-Waste Management in Ghana.* Freiburg, Germany: Öko-Institut e.V.

Rashna, R. R., and S. M. Naureen M. 2015. "Electronic Waste: The story of Bangladesh." *The Daily Star.* mhttps://www.thedailystar.net/op-ed/politics/electronic-waste-the-story-bangladesh-121792

Sepulveda, A., M. Schluep., F. B. Renauld., M. Streicher., R. Kuehr, C. Hagelüken, A. C. Gerecke. 2010. "A Review of the Environmental Fate and Effects of Hazardous Substances Released from Electrical and Electronic Equipment during the Recycling: Examples from China and India." *Environmental Impact Assessment Review* 30, no. 1, pp. 28–41.

Sheikh, I. 2017. "Recycling E-Waste." *The Independent.* mhttp://www.theindependentbd.com/printversion/details/120764

Tanskanen, P. 2013. Management and Recycling of Electronic Waste. *Acta Materialia* 61, no. 3, pp. 1001–11.

The Daily Observer. 2017. "E-Waste Management Rules – 2017." mhttp://www.observerbd.com/details.php?id=104758

The Independent. 2018. "E-Waste Management." http://www.theindependentbd.com/arcprint/details/146352/2018-04-19

Thomas, L., and P. Revoir. 2010. "Computers and TV Take Up Half Our Lives as We Spend Seven Hours a Day Using Technology." *Dailymail.* mhttp://www.dailymail.co.uk/news/article-1304266/We-spend-7-hours-day-using-technology-computers-TV-lives.html#ixzz3ySZCFWnH

Tsydenova, O., and M. Bengtsson. 2011. "Chemical Hazards Associated with Treatment of Waste Electrical and Electronic Equipment." *Waste Management* 31, no. 1, pp. 45–58.

UNB Dhaka. 2017. "UNIDO to help Bangladesh Manage E-Waste." *The Daily Star.* mhttps://www.thedailystar.net/city/unido-help-bangladesh-manage-e-waste-1458346

United Nations Sustainable Development Programme. n.d. "Transforming the World: The 2030 Agenda of Sustainable Development." https://sustainabledevelopment.un.org/post2015/transformingourworld

Acts and Policy

Bangladesh Bio-safety Rules 2012.

Bangladesh Environment Conservation Act 2010.

Bangladesh Environment Conservation Policy 2010.

Bangladesh Environment Protection Act 2010.

Bangladesh Hazardous Waste and Ship Breaking Waste Management Policy 2011.

Bangladesh Import Policy Order 2015-2018.

Bangladesh National Environment Policy 1992.

Bangladesh Sound Pollution Policy 2006.

Chemical Substance Depleting Ozone Layer (Control) Policy 2004.

Director General, Environment, 2006. "Guidance on the Interpretation of Key Provisions of Directive 2008/98/EC on Waste".

The Basel Convention, 1989.

The Basel Convention, 1993.

The Environmental Conservation Rules, 1997 of Bangladesh.

The Environmental Court Act 2000 of Bangladesh.

The Waste Electrical and Electronic Equipment Directive (2002/96/EC) 2002.

The Waste Electrical and Electronic Equipment Directive (2012/19/EU) 2012.

CHAPTER 8

Disasters and Medicinal and Aromatic Plants (MAPs)

Preparing Governance for Resilient MAP-based Livelihood in Uttarakhand

Vinay Sharma
Pramod Chandra
Rajat Agrawal

Department of Management Studies, Indian Institute of Technology Roorkee, Roorkee, Uttarakhand, India

Introduction

Around the world the medicinal and aromatic plants (MAPs) are extensively traded and considered as an essential commodity for producing various herbal-based products including herbal drugs (Lubbe and Verpoorte 2011). As a result, these resources have become a vital source of livelihood and employment for many rural communities in the biodiversity-rich regions of the world. In the Indian context, the domain and role of MAPs in the form of herbal remedies and formulations for various health conditions is accessible with scientific validity in different traditional Indian scriptures and Vedic literature (i.e., Sushruta Samhita, Rig Veda, Atharva Veda, Charaka Samhita, Bhela Samhita, and the medical part of the Bower Manuscript) (Loukas et al. 2010; Raju 2003; Zimmerman and Veith 1961).

The legacy of MAPs in India is largely maintained in the Indian Himalayan Region (IHR). The IHR contributes around 1,748 recognized species of valuable MAPs, which is 32.2 percent of India's MAPs (Chandra and Sharma 2018). Uttarakhand in IHR is endowed with rich diversity of MAPs and represents nearly 40.10 percent MAPs of IHR (Kuniyal et al. 2015; Samant and Pal 2003). The inherent biodiversity of Uttarakhand is primarily attributed to its suitable geo-climatic conditions and unique landscape of the region. Geographically, Uttarakhand is situated on the south slope of Himalayan ranges, which varies from glaciers in the high mountains to tropical forest at lower altitude and forms different types of landscapes and climatic conditions. The ancient scriptures of India on medicine and medical science also describe the Himalayan region as a suitable habitat and veritable emporium of MAPs (Aswal 1993; Rautela 1998).

The Government of India has declared Uttarakhand as the "Herbal State" in the year 2003 to acknowledge the rich availability of MAPs and the herbal heritage of Uttarakhand (Sati 2013) and classified 132 species of MAPs (indigenous and exotic) as substantial for the socioeconomic development of the state (Kuniyal et al. 2015). Presently, 701 species of MAPs are officially recorded and recognized in Uttarakhand (Bisht, Negi, and Bhandari 2016), out of which 28 species are categorized as "globally significant medicinal plants" (GSMP) (Kuniyal et al. 2015; Kuniyal and Sundriyal 2013; Ved and Goraya 2008) by the state government with an objective of cultivation and conservation from socioeconomic as well as sustainability perspective.

Role of MAPs in Livelihood and Economy

The rich biodiversity of Uttarakhand offers a wide range of livelihood opportunities for the dwellers (Ram 2003). The opportunities are predominantly connected to agriculture, commercialization of forest-based products, fodder, alternative source of energy, and trade in MAPs. Particularly, the trade and commercialization of MAPs signifies a substantial role in the household income of many rural communities in the region. It has been estimated that 17 percent to 35 percent of household income of the rural communities in Uttarakhand comes through trade and sales of MAPs (Chauhan 2010). The trade of MAPs, in the form of wild harvested MAPs, is also a profitable source of revenue generation for the state government. In the year 2005 to 2006 the sales of MAPs from the forests of

Uttarakhand had generated US$255.535 million, whereas up to March 2012 to 2013, it has grown up to US$402.674 million (UAFDC 2017).

However, despite the huge potential of MAPs for revenue generation, socioeconomic development, and uplift of rural communities, the MAP sector of Uttarakhand is facing diverse issues such as trade and marketing problems (Chandra and Sharma 2018; Kuniyal et al. 2013). Also, the absence of a planning framework for managing the resource base in the event of natural disasters is causing vulnerable conditions for the sustainability of MAP resources in Uttarakhand. This is consequently creating challenging situations for the livelihood of many rural communities but yet not discussed in academic or scientific literature.

Objectives of the Study

To instigate a conversation on the impact of various disasters on MAPs diversity in Uttarakhand in the academic literature and debates, this chapter primarily focuses on the following objectives:

1. To analyze the role of various institutions such as research and development institutes, commercial organizations, nongovernmental organizations, self-help groups, community organizations etc. in promoting the conservation and management of MAPs in the occurrence of any sort of disasters;
2. To revisit the major disasters and the impact on the existence of the MAPs in Uttarakhand;
3. To analyze policy gaps and its impact on natural resources in Uttarakhand;
4. To consider the impact of information gaps on the loss of the valuable species of MAPs.

Literature Review

In contemporary literature, no specific research studies are available on the impact of different disasters on MAPs diversity and the livelihood of associated communities. Therefore, major studies that describe how the disastrous events affect agriculture have been included in this study, because the MAPs are allied to agriculture.

Disasters and Natural Resources

The Food and Agriculture Organization of the United Nations (FAO 2018), in its report, *The Impact of Disasters on Agriculture and Food Security 2017*, stated that "Disasters jeopardize agricultural production and development and often have cascading negative effects across national economies" (p. iii). The report categorically admits the adverse consequence of disasters on agriculture.

Similar to the impact of disasters on agriculture, any sort of disastrous situation poses serious threats for the existence of MAPs resources by habitat destruction and change in landscape, which consequently lead to the extinction of valuable MAP resources. The extinction of MAPs means the loss of raw materials to the pharmaceutical industries and the loss of livelihood for the inhabitants of the community.

Natural disasters pose major negative impact on agriculture and crop production and therefore there must be some national-level planning framework that could effectively reduce the impact of problems posed by disastrous situations (Lesk, Rowhani, and Ramankutty 2016; Long 1978). The re-occurrence of natural disasters will be a major threat for sustainable agriculture in the next decade, which will consequently challenge the competitiveness of the sector (Klomp and Hoogezand 2018). Particularly in mountain ecosystems, like Uttarakhand, the frequently occurring disasters are of dire consequence with the loss of numerous biodiversity resources. For the past several years Uttarakhand has been the victim of some major disasters, like the disaster of Kedarnath in 2013 and the massive forest fire of 2016. Such disasters badly affected the lives and resources of the state. But, unfortunately, no information is available about the impact of these disasters on MAPs' sustainability in Uttarakhand. This illustrates the need to fill the information gaps when a disastrous happens. The loss of livelihood of the local community resulting from the disasters needs to be studied.

Methodology

After a careful consideration of the ontological and epistemological aspects associated with the MAPs sector in Uttarakhand, the post-positivist research philosophy is adopted to pursue this study. The ontological and epistemological considerations have led the authors to choose the qualitative reflexive methodology (Alvesson and Sköldberg 2017) to understand the diverse aspects that eventually shape the sustainability and livelihood in the MAPs sector in Uttarakhand. Therefore, experience of one of the authors of this chapter associated with the MAP sector of Uttarakhand has been utilized to focus the study on the disastrous situations and the resulting impact on the sustainability of MAP resources and on the livelihood of associated communities. Further to achieving the objectives, the required information has been collected through reviewing the literature about the impact of disasters on the agriculture sector and reflexive interpretations have been made, because hardly any literature is available about the impact of disasters on the MAPs, to comprehend the impact of disasters on MAPs sector of Uttarakhand. Subsequently, after careful understanding of the impact of disasters on agriculture similar aspects have also been recognized in the MAPs sector in Uttarakhand. Finally, based on the understanding developed through the reflexive approach, the required strategies and recommendations are proposed in this chapter.

The related literature was reviewed between 2016 and 2017 and some unstructured interviews were also conducted, in the beginning of 2017, with individuals who were the victims of disasters in Uttarakhand and its consequential effects on their livelihood. The experiences of the victims were intensely recognized in the reflexive interpretation of the situation.

Analysis and Discussion

Institutions Working for the Management of the MAPs in Uttarakhand

Various institutions and agencies in Uttarakhand (Table 8.1) are working in the development of MAPs sector (Kuniyal et al. 2015). The common functional areas of these institutions include the research and developmental activities for MAPs resources; facilitating farmers and interest groups in cultivation; providing marketing and commercialization platform for the growers and harvesters through authorized trade channels; and activities for livelihood enhancement through the MAP sector. However, the threat to sustainability of MAPs as a consequence of disasters are not acknowledged as an area of concern by these groups. Therefore, the conservation of the MAPs in ordinary circumstances is properly managed, but in the case of any occurring disaster the existence and/or the management of MAPs becomes challenging. Which consequently, hinders the livelihood of many rural communities.

Table 8.1 Various institutions working for the management of medicinal and aromatic plants sector in Uttarakhand

S.N.	Name of the institutions
1	State Medicinal Plant Board (SMPB)
2	Herbal Research & Development Institute (HRDI)
3	Uttarakhand Forest Development Corporation (UAFDC)
4	Centre for Aromatic Plants (CAP)
5	High Altitude Plant Physiology Research Centre (HAPPRC)
6	National Medicinal Plants Board (NMPB)
7	G.B. Pant National Institute of Himalayan Environment & Sustainable Development (GBPNIHESD)
8	United Nations Development Programme ( ) and various nongovernmental organizations and cooperatives

Source: Compiled by authors.

Major Disasters of Uttarakhand and Their Impact on Natural Resources

The geography and ecosystem of Uttarakhand is very sensitive (Kala 2014; Kuniyal 2013); therefore, it always remains vulnerable to various kinds of disasters as seen in the disasters of Kedarnath in 2013 (Sharma, Joshi, and Agrawal 2015) and the massive forest fire of 2016 (Table 8.2). Experts have estimated that the total loss of the land and resources is still uncountable, and these disasters have washed-out numerous natural resources and destroyed the landscape in various ecologically sensitive zones of the state. Thus, this creates a need to document and monitor important natural resources (i.e., MAPs) for their sustainability and long-term existence.

Table 8.2 List of major disasters in Uttarakhand

Year	Disasters
1978	Landslides at Kanoliya Gaad in Uttarkashi
1980	Cloudburst at Gayansu village
1991	Earthquake in Uttarkashi district
1998	Landslide in Mansoona village
1998	Landslide in Pithoragarh district
1999	Earthquake in Chamoli district
2002	Landslide in Budha Kedar
2003	Landslide in Varunavat and Uttarkashi districts
2010	Cloudburst and landslide in Uttarkashi, Chamoli and Rudraprayag districts
2012	Cloudburst in Assiganga and Bhagirathi Valley, Uttarkashi
2012	Landslide in Ukkimath and Rudraprayag districts
2013	Kedarnath disaster
2016	Massive forest fire

Source: Indpaedia (2015) and compiled by authors.

Policy Gap and Natural Resources in Uttarakhand

The absence of tangible policy framework for mitigating the impact of disasters on MAPs sector of Uttarakhand is another key issue affecting the sustainability of the MAPs and livelihood of the rural communities. For example, the excessive fall of pine needles is usually considered a major cause of forest fires in the higher forests of Uttarakhand. As a result, the Himalayan ecosystem is steadily deteriorating (Joshi, Sharma, and Mittal 2015). Likewise, the strict legal regulations in Uttarakhand also prohibit the public participation in conservational measures (Joshi, Sharma, and Mittal 2015) of MAPs and hence community participation is also missing in the conservation of resources. It is also calculated that about 50 percent of the forests of India are vulnerable to forest fire (DTE 2016). On the other hand, the forests are the major sources of MAPs as about 90 percent of these plants are harvested from the wild. Therefore, proper measures should be implemented to prevent and minimize the impact of forest fires on MAPs.

Information Gap and Its Impact on MAPs Diversity in Disastrous Situations

Information gaps, as highlighted by FAO (n.d.) for agriculture sector in the situation of disasters, are similarly evident for the MAPs sector in Uttarakhand. The MAPs sector of Uttarakhand is witnessing a huge data gap at global, national, and regional levels in order to mitigate the impact of disasters on MAPs sustainability and livelihood of the associated communities. As a consequence, the information gap is leading the absence of quantifiable information on the number of MAPs that are vulnerable to the occurrence of disasters in particular areas of the state.

The report of FAO focuses on strengthening the regional and global database and information system to capture the extent and impact of disasters on the sector. The non-standardization process of data collection is leading to the understanding of the criticality of disastrous events for the MAPs sector. The regular monitoring and reporting of the existence of the MAPs and the impact of disasters is the need of the hour. The systematic collection and monitoring of the damage information is also critical for measuring the impact of disasters on the MAPs sector. In order to meet the above challenges, the necessary interventions are urgently required as a part of policy and information to tackle the loss and damage of this important resource and for the long-term sustainability of the MAPs. This is important as they are not only required to meet the needs of the contemporary herbal market, but they are equally important for the ecosystem and livelihood requirement of many rural communities.

Recommendations

Policy Intervention Required for Resilient MAP-based Livelihoods in Uttarakhand

In order to reduce or mitigate the impact of disasters on MAPs, especially in the areas where disasters cause heavy loss to natural resources, it is necessary to address the following guidelines. These guidelines are in line with FAO guidelines for mitigating the impact of disasters on agriculture and natural resources.

A) Disasters risk reduction for resilience building in medicinal plants based livelihood is essential in Uttarakhand, therefore it should be a priority for government and private stakeholders to invest in the sector for resilience activities.

B) The disaster risk reduction and management, which is considered as a backbone of resilience, must be systematically entrenched into the MAPs sector and its development, as it is an important source of livelihood, and is a key driver of economic well-being of many mountain communities.

C) The activities and strategies of disaster risk reduction must be integrated with the post-disaster recovery efforts in the MAPs sector to ensure the investment made in the disaster response and recovery also to build resilience for future disasters.

D) The state regime along with the support of national and global institutions must find the ways for financing the disaster risk reduction program in the MAPs sector of Uttarakhand in order to prevent and mitigate the future impact of disasters on MAPs.

Framework for Preparing Governance for Resilient MAP-based Livelihoods in Uttarakhand

To prepare the governance for resilient MAP-based livelihood in Uttarakhand, the following framework is proposed (Figure 8.1). The proposed framework primarily focuses on four key aspects, which are initially required for the resilience of MAP-based livelihood and sustainable development of MAPs in Uttarakhand,

A) The government must initiate buffer plantations in barren land. In Uttarakhand a large area of land is under government control and is suitable as a natural habitat for a plantation of MAPs. Therefore, that land could be used for growing the diversity of MAPs, which consequently will increase the production and the options of livelihood for rural communities.

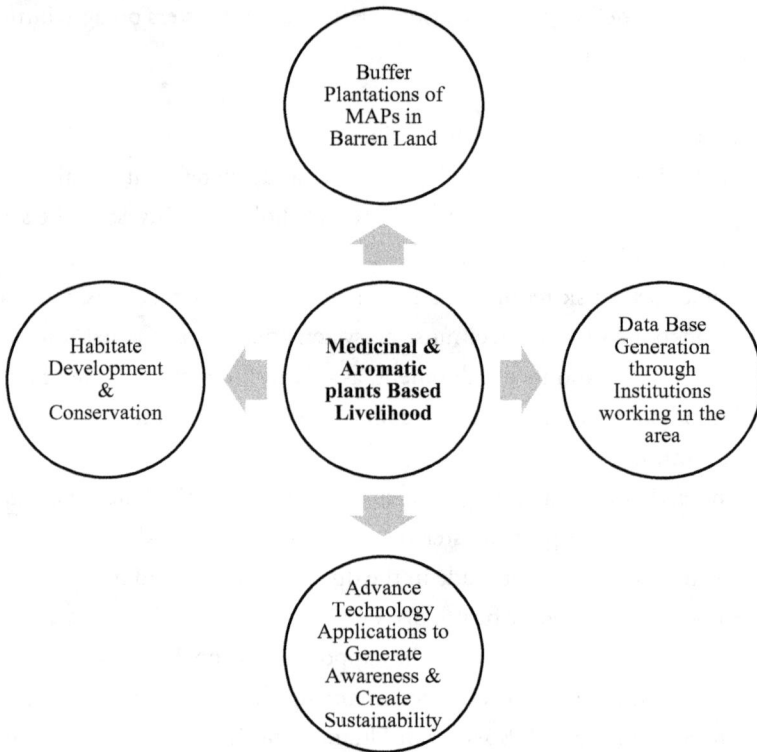

Figure 8.1 **A framework for preparing governance for resilient MAP-based livelihoods in Uttarakhand**

Source: The authors.

B) The government can also conserve and develop the already existing habitats of the MAPs, which will preserve the obliteration activities near the habitats.

C) A substantial database must be generated with the help of various stakeholders working for the development of MAPs in Uttarakhand. The database is extremely useful in mitigating the impact of disasters and planning the livelihood resilience activities in the MAPs sector in Uttarakhand.

D) The fourth key element of the framework is application of advance information technology tools to generate awareness among communities about the impact of disasters on the resources and motivating them for sustainability measures.

Conclusion

This chapter offers an initial attempt to preparing a system of governance for a resilient MAP-based livelihood in Uttarakhand along with exemplifying the impact of various disasters on the sustainability of MAPs resources and livelihood of native communities. However, the policy framework, which is presently operative in the MAPs sector of Uttarakhand, has a substantial strategy and information gap in terms of disaster risk reduction and the management of MAP resources. In particular, the policy and information gaps are creating several challenges for MAP sustainability and livelihood of the native communities.

To address the issues, the roles of various institutions engaged in the management of MAP resources were examined, then the sort of disasters that are frequently creating issues for the resource base and human survival in Uttarakhand and how the present policy structure is ineffective to tackle the situation have been discussed. Finally, the consequence of the information gap in the situation of disasters and post-disasters mitigations planning is also discussed in this chapter. The analysis was, however, limited by the absence of consistent information on the impact of disasters on MAPs' sustainability and livelihood of rural communities in Uttarakhand. The study therefore sets the grounds for future disasters-related studies that are necessary for preparing a system of governance for resilient MAP-based livelihood and resources sustainability in the context of any sort of disaster. Thus, this study asserts that an immediate strategic intervention in the policy framework of MAPs of Uttarakhand to align it with disaster risk and mitigation for sustainable resources management and livelihood of rural communities associated with the sector is necessary.

References

Alvesson, M., and K. Sköldberg. 2017. *Reflexive Methodology: New Vistas for Qualitative Research*. New Delhi, India: Sage.

Aswal, B. S. 1993. "Rare or Threatened Medicinal Plants of Garhwal Himalaya and Their Conservation." In *Garhwal Himalaya Ecology and Environment*, ed. G. S. Rajwar, pp. 99–105. New Delhi, India: Ashish Publishing House.

Bisht, V. K., J. S. Negi, and A. K. Bhandari. 2016. "Check on Extinction of Medicinal Herbs in Uttarakhand: No Need to Uproot." *National Academy Science Letters* 39, no. 3, pp. 233–35.

Chandra, P., and V. Sharma. 2018. "Strategic Marketing Prospects for Developing Sustainable Medicinal and Aromatic Plants Businesses in the Indian Himalayan Region." *Small-scale Forestry*, pp. 1–19.

Chauhan, R. S. 2010. "Socioeconomic Improvement through Medicinal and Aromatic Plants (MAPs) Cultivation in Uttarakhand, India." *Journal of Sustainable Agriculture* 34, no. 6, pp. 647–58.

DTE (Down to Earth). 2016. "Fire in the Mountains." http://www.downtoearth.org.in/blog/fire-in-the-mountains-53885

FAO (The Food and Agriculture Organization). 2018. *The Impact of Disasters on Agriculture and Food Security 2017.* http://www.fao.org/3/I8656EN/i8656en.pdf

FAO. n. d. *The Forest Biodiversity Challenge.* http://www.fao.org/fileadmin/templates/rap/files/NRE/Forestry_Group/3_Forest_biodiversity.pdf

Indpaedia. 2015. *Uttarakhand: Natural Disasters–A History of Disasters.* http://indpaedia.com/ind/index.php/Uttarakhand: Natural disasters

Joshi, K., V. Sharma, and S. Mittal. 2015. "Social Entrepreneurship through Forest Bioresidue Briquetting: An Approach to Mitigate Forest Fires in Pine Areas of Western Himalaya, India." *Renewable and Sustainable Energy Reviews* 51, pp. 1338–44.

Kala, C. P. 2014. "Deluge, Disaster and Development in Uttarakhand Himalayan Region of India: Challenges and Lessons for Disaster Management." *International Journal of Disaster Risk Reduction* 8, pp. 143–52.

Klomp, J., and B. Hoogezand. 2018. "Natural Disasters and Agricultural Protection: A Panel Data Analysis." *World Development* 104, pp. 404–17.

Kuniyal, C. P. 2013. "Sustainable Mountain Development in Indian Himalayan Region Is under the Shadow of Regional Instability." *Current Science* 105, no. 3, p. 293.

Kuniyal, C. P., and R. C. Sundriyal. 2013. "Conservation Salvage of Cordyceps Sinensis Collection in the Himalayan Mountains Is Neglected." *Ecosystem Services* 3, pp. e40–43.

Kuniyal, C. P., P. C. Kuniyal, J. S. Butola, and R. C. Sundriyal. 2013. "Trends in the Marketing of Some Important Medicinal Plants in Uttarakhand, India." *International Journal of Biodiversity Science, Ecosystem Services & Management* 9, no. 4, pp. 324–29.

Kuniyal, C. P., V. K. Bisht, J. S. Negi, V. P. Bhatt, D. S. Bisht, J. S. Butola, R. C. Sundriyal, and S. K. Singh. 2015. "Progress and Prospect in the Integrated Development of Medicinal and Aromatic Plants (MAPs) Sector in Uttarakhand, Western Himalaya." *Environment, Development and Sustainability* 17, no. 5, pp. 1141–62.

Lesk, C., P. Rowhani and N. Ramankutty. 2016. "Influence of Extreme Weather Disasters on Global Crop Production." *Nature* 529, no. 7584, pp. 84–87.

Long, F. 1978. "The Impact of Natural Disasters on Third World Agriculture: An Exploratory Survey of the Need for Some New Dimensions in Development Planning." *American Journal of Economics and Sociology* 37, no. 2, pp. 149–63.

Loukas, M., A. Lanteri, J. Ferrauiola, R. S. Tubbs, G. Maharaja, M. M. Shoja, A. Yadav and V. C. Rao. 2010. "Anatomy in Ancient India: A Focus on the Susruta Samhita." *Journal of Anatomy* 217, no. 6, pp. 646–50.

Lubbe, A., and R. Verpoorte. 2011. "Cultivation of Medicinal and Aromatic Plants for Specialty Industrial Materials." *Industrial Crops and Products* 34, no. 1, pp. 785–801.

Raju, V. K. 2003. "Susruta of Ancient India." *Indian Journal of Ophthalmology* 5, no. 2, p. 119.

Ram, J., A. Kumar, and A. B. Bhatt. 2003. *Plant Biodiversity of Uttaranchal, Central Himalayan Forests, India*. Almora, India: GB Pant Institute of Himalayan Environment and Development.

Rautela, N. 1998. "Medicinal Herbs of the Himalaya: A Threat to Their Survival." In *Mountain Ecosystems: A Scenario of Unsustainability*, eds. V. Singh and M. L. Sharma, pp. 182–85. New Delhi, India: Indus Publishing Company.

Samant, S. S., and M. Pal. 2003. "Diversity and Conservation Status of Medicinal Plants in Uttaranchal State." *Indian Forester* 129, no. 9, pp. 1090–108.

Sati, V. P. 2013. "Cultivation of Medicinal Plants and Its Contribution to Livelihood Enhancement in the Indian Central Himalayan Region." *Advancement in Medicinal Plant Research* 1, no. 2, pp. 17–23.

Sharma, V., K. K. Joshi, and R. Agrawal. 2015. "Mitigating Disasters through Community Involvement and Righteous Practices in Himalayan Region of Uttarakhand, India." In *Strategic Disaster Risk Management in Asia*, eds. H. Ha, R. L. S. Fernando, and A. Mahmood, pp. 99–114. New Delhi, India: Springer.

UAFDC (Uttarakhand Forest Development Corporation). 2017. *Achievements-Year wise Detail of Sales of Zari Booty.* http://www.uafdc.in/achievments.html

Ved, D. K., and G. S. Goraya. 2008. *Demand and Supply of Medicinal Plants in India.* Devon, UK: Bishen Singh Mahendra Pal Singh.

Zimmerman, L. M., and I. Veith. 1961. *Great Ideas in the History of Surgery.* pp. 101–105. Baltimore, MD: Williams & Wilkins.

CHAPTER 9

Practical Knowledge in High School Students—Sufficient for Disaster Readiness or Not

The Bangladesh Perspective

Md Zahir Ahmed
Policy Research Centre, Dhaka

Akbaruddin Ahmad
Policy Research Centre, Dhaka

Oli Ahmed
Department of Psychology, University of Chittagong, Chittagong

Introduction

Bangladesh is a natural disaster–prone country of an area about 1,47,570 sq. km with population over 160 million (Ministry of Finance 2015) with a population growth of 1.18 percent (Worldometers 2017). Bangladesh is one of the most densely populated countries of the world. The population density here is 1,077/km^2 (Ministry of Finance 2015). Due to its geographic and geologic setting it has a long history of both natural and man-made disasters such as floods, cyclones, droughts, tidal surges, tornadoes, river erosion, high arsenic content in ground water, water-logging, soil salinity, fire, collapse of buildings, and many more. Disasters cause massive misfortune to people through death, injuries, harm to properties, livelihood, and financial circumstances. The country faces at least one major disaster a year. Bangladesh is one of the most vulnerable countries due to climate change because of its geo-location. Loss of property and lives from natural calamities is very common in Bangladesh. Adopting with, the way Bangladesh is adopting with this massive problem is unique. Bangladesh has the lack of all sorts of resources to cope with climate change and natural disasters but is blessed with the resilience of people. Because of this community resilience, Bangladesh has become a role model in adopting with the disasters to the world. But this is the era of sustainable development in terms of disaster management (DM), so textbook knowledge is a must go alongside the resilience. In countries like Bangladesh, DM is mostly done by the local and community volunteers and this huge portion completely comes from students. To make this effective working force more efficient, it is very important to give them proper training and education. For providing the training, the Government of the People's Republic of Bangladesh has the program of developing urban community volunteers. With the cooperation and supervision of Fire Service & Civil Defense (FSCD), Government of Bangladesh has developed 62,000 volunteers of this kind. But this program is only for the urban areas so to cover all the areas alternative method is required.

Addressing the importance of having disaster risk reduction (DRR) knowledge, we are considering the textbook knowledge so important for the world's one of the most disaster-prone areas. It has lost on average 3.02 percent of its gross domestic product (GDP) every year during the last 10 years and holds the highest disaster mortality rate in the world (see Figure 9.1).

With a per capita income of US$1,602 (www.mof.gov.bd), Bangladesh experiences a very high physical and social vulnerability. Most of the dense areas are noted for lower socioeconomic conditions along with being disaster-prone as well. Climate change along with the unethical and criminal activities of some immoral people add a new dimension to community risks and vulnerabilities. As a result, Bangladesh now sits at the top of the global climate risk index.

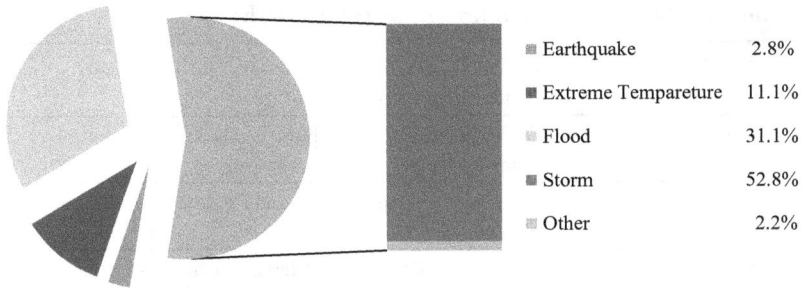

▦ Earthquake	2.8%
▪ Extreme Tempareture	11.1%
▨ Flood	31.1%
▪ Storm	52.8%
▨ Other	2.2%

Figure 9.1 Internationally reported losses 1990 to 2014 of Bangladesh by disasters

Source: Basic Country Statistics and Indicators (Prevention Web 2015).

Study Background

The Ministry of Education placed emphasis on climate change studies along with the DM and DRR. There has been a notable focus on DM and climate change in the 2010 National Education Policy. In all levels of education, the policy has broadened the study and research on the disaster and climate change issue. According to the policy principle no. 18 of National Education Policy 2010 by the Ministry of Education, Government of People's Republic of Bangladesh:

> to build student as skilled human resources to fight the challenges of the world threatened by climate change and other natural disasters and to create in them a social awareness about environment. (Government of People's Republic of Bangladesh 2010)

According to the National Disaster Management and Disaster Risk Reduction strategy, Bangladesh has merged its educational curriculum with DRR education. It has an exceptional and intensive school education module with similar reading materials being utilized across the country. The National Curriculum and Text Book Board (NCTB) has presented disaster and environmental change–related topics (i.e., hazards, vulnerability, preparedness) inside parts in various different course books, for example, Bangla, English, Social Science, General Science. The examples of topics included in lessons in primary schools and high schools are in Table 9.1, and examples of topics included in textbooks are in Table 9.2.

Table 9.1 Disaster-related lessons in Bangladesh

Primary level education	Natural environment with emphasize on topics like climate change
Ibtedaye level (Madrasa)	Environment Science with the inclusion of the concept "climate change"
High School level	Included the climate change and DRR issue in all classes of high school
Higher level education	The subject climate change has a new horizon for higher studies
Agricultural Studies	Undertaking intensive research on agriculture development in the context of the threat of climate change, initiative will be taken for research on high-yielding seeds, climate change, agriculture, and biotechnology

Source: Government of Bangladesh (2010).

Table 9.2 Disaster-related lessons in the textbooks of high school

S/No.	Class	Subject	Topic
1	Class 6	Science	Definitions of disasters, classifications of different types of disasters, planning for disaster mitigation
		English for Today	Water crisis, floods
2	Class 7	General Science	Floods, river bank erosion and drought in Bangladesh
3	Class 8	General Science	Natural disaster—cyclones and tidal surges (Islam, undated)
4		Bangladesh o Bisshoporichoy (Bangladesh & Introduction to the world) (A textbook for Grade 8)	Global warming—cause and effect, concept of disasters and types, brief discussion on disaster management (DM) and DRR
5	Classes 9–10	Geography	Natural disasters of Bangladesh; disaster and hazard, types and effects of disasters, DM and DRR, impact of disaster, prevention–mitigation–preparedness–recovery and development for disaster
6		Science	Effect of climate change, cause of environmental problems, cause–prevention–strategies–measures of disasters, conservation of nature, social awareness for prevention of disasters

Source: National Curriculum and Textbook Board, Ministry of Education, Bangladesh (2017).

Lessons inside reading material are frequently refreshed and checked on by the NCTB to make them more hazard administration situated. Considering there are four distinctive geo-climatic zones in Bangladesh and that diverse districts are influenced by various types of risks (for instance, drought in the north; cyclones and tidal surges in the south, waterway disintegration and flooding in the central area). Given these regional distinctions, it is extremely sketchy whether course textbooks can adaptably address specific provincial and local perils. Thus, one must question the practical knowledge on DM and DRR being presented to students to gain effective learning outcomes and competencies among the high school students.

Research Question and the Objectives of the Study

The present study aimed to find an answer for the level of adequacy of DM-related knowledge in high school textbooks in the Bangladesh school system. To be more specific, the research questions are:

1. Is the knowledge within high school textbooks adequate for disaster readiness?
2. Is there any correlation between gender and residential difference for DRR and DM knowledge?

The present work studied the relevance and adequacy of the practical knowledge on DM and DRR among high school students with the immediate association and legitimate connection with their textual knowledge. Other objectives of the study were as follows:

1. To assess whether the level of disaster-related knowledge from curriculum-based textbook knowledge is sufficient or not for awareness and readiness.
2. Whether gender is a factor in any differences in disaster-related knowledge, readiness, and awareness.
3. Whether residential area is a factor in any differences in disaster-related knowledge, readiness, and awareness.
4. To find out more effective ways to promote disaster readiness related knowledge among high school students.

Significance of the Study

The findings of the present study question the ability of the country to adapt to disasters and disaster resilience strength by assessing the knowledge in high school students. From the general public in disaster-prone nations, there is an interest in community volunteers as the principal responders. In such manner, students are given to make up a significant portion of the main functional team, so having sound knowledge of DM is essential for the high school students to ensure effective disaster resilience. Thus, authorities that apply the recommended approach derived from the results of this study will be able to know the actual knowledge outcomes for the high school students toward DM. Educationists and education policy makers will be guided on what should be emphasized to include or modify in the textbooks regarding DM and resilience. For the researcher/s, the study will help them uncover critical areas regarding students that many researchers were not able to explore. Thus, a new horizon of DM knowledge, which is actually directly connected to the disaster resilience, may be arrived at.

Literature Review

DRR in the worldwide setting that is molded by the Hyogo Framework of Action, which was received by 168 member nations in 2005. Need three of its five focuses says the system is to "use knowledge, innovation, and education to build a culture of safety and resilience at all levels" (United Nations International Strategy for Disaster Reduction 2005, p. 22). As a cost-effective approach, necessity of the DRR has been recognized by Bangladesh to improve the level of preparedness, response, recovery, and rehabilitation in disaster-prone areas (Disaster Management Bureau 2010).

In 2010, the Government of Bangladesh prepared a five-year national plan for DM. To reduce the risk of disaster-prone areas' both types of disasters (natural calamities and man-made hazards), an emergency response system for handling these disasters was established. A core emphasis of this plan was to increase the awareness of the people and make preparedness strategies consistent with community involvement.

As an important medium to increase the awareness to disaster preparedness and an effective way to communicate the plan, the National

Education Policy (National Curriculum and Textbook Board, Ministry of Education, Bangladesh 2010) by the Government of Bangladesh included disaster preparedness among its 30 aims and objectives for national education. Disaster readiness was introduced in 2004. The National Curriculum and Textbook Board introduced disaster and climate change–related chapters within textbooks in a range of subjects at various grade levels after the announcement by the Ministry of Education in 2014 that disaster preparedness would be integrated in more texts. As textbooks are written well and covered a large amount of material, the approach spearheaded by NCTB raises a number of important issues (Kagawa and Selby 2014). The questions related to access to disaster readiness curriculum indicates the question of vertical curricular progression. The chapters of the textbooks do not convey any sense of considered development and deepening of understanding of disaster risk through the grade levels (Kagawa and Selby 2014). There is lack of sequence and continuity to the content of disaster readiness grade by grade. There are some themes that are taught at primary level as well as in the secondary level. So, a question arises about the sufficiency of knowledge in textbooks. However, Chowdhury, Sarwar, and Muhibullah (2013) suggested that it is not necessarily a problem, but progression must be there in terms of complexity and scope, which are related to students' maturity and prior knowledge and understanding. For example, the cyclone poem in the grade 5 Bangla language textbook is not embedded in DRR understanding; it is just a poem (Kagawa and Selby 2014). If we take a quick view to the textbooks and compare these with other topics in these textbooks, we may identify these as standing in islands of knowledge disconnected from a framework of disaster readiness learning outcomes. This is true both through the grade levels and between subjects.

Conveyed knowledge and information through the use of textbooks is organized within the restrictive confines of traditional academic disciplines with an emphasis on what matters to each discipline. The approach is multidisciplinary that one is applying the lens of a variety of subjects to disaster readiness but falling short to consider how the learning from each subject relates to and raises learning challenges within other subjects (Selby and Kagawa 2012). It appears that writers and contributors of NCTB's textbooks are wedded to a narrow and traditional view of a general education program rather than taking to heart the demands of education for sustainable development' (Chowdhury, Sarwar, and Muhibullah 2013). Another problem is that schools in Bangladesh emphasize in memorization and getting good grade. So, it presents challenges to disaster-related readiness program knowledge in textbooks related to application of that knowledge in practical life. If we cannot apply our gathered knowledge to our life, it will be considered as insufficient knowledge.

Chowdhury (2017) conducted a study in Dhaka city, Bangladesh, on disaster preparedness. This research aimed to analyze disaster preparedness in both prepared policies by the government and practices related to urban hazards in Dhaka city. Researcher in this study examined the role of government and different nongovernmental organizations (NGOs) to implement the policies. It was recommended that success of the policies and strategies implemented by government depended on proper and efficient monitoring and implementation. To reduce the cost of hazards, proper mechanism should be introduced in both organizational and individual levels.

Methodology

Sample Size and the Target Group

Since the study was aiming to focus on the adequacy of DRR knowledge in the high school textbooks, so we did not go for the random sampling. In this regard, we have found quota sampling as the best suits. These specific subgroups were the high schools students. Besides, we have focused on the gender and residential differences. The sample comprised 400 high school students. They were selected, as sample, purposively on the basis of two basic criteria. The first and absolute one was the gender (e.g., boy and girl), the next one was the residence (e.g., urban and rural). Since DM and DRR is all about the community engagement, so we emphasized on levels 8, 9, and 10. We did not use levels 6 and 7 due to the maturity issue on the textual knowledge. If we illustrate the sample in statistical way, then 50 percent (200) respondents were from urban area and 50 percent (200) of rural. On the gender basis, 50 percent (200) were boys and 50 percent (200) girls. Among the boys, 40 percent (80) were from class 8, 30 percent (60) from class 9, and 30 percent (60) from class 10. The overall statistics of boys and girls were identical. Their age ranged from 13 years to 17 years.

Instrument

To gather necessary information for the present study, the Bangla of DRR and DM Knowledge Questionnaire for High School Students (Tuladhar et al. 2014) was used. To make it more representable to Bangladeshi perspective, it is so composed that one section of it consists of four quantitative and one qualitative items, which were systematically adopted and included in the main measure as well. The questionnaire was in Bangla, and it went through proper back translation process.

DM Knowledge Scale for High School Students

DRR and DM Knowledge Scale for high school students comprises five sections. The very first one is entitled Disaster-Related Concerns, which has three items or statements. The next section is Readiness Behavior with seven items; the next one is Adaptation with Disasters with seven items. The following section is Disaster Awareness with seven items and the last section is entitled Disaster Risk Preparedness, which has four items. For each item, the respondents were asked to indicate their responses at three possible levels: Yes, No and Don't Know.

Additional Section

To make the measure more conceptualized with the study, an additional section entitled Textual Knowledge was adopted with four quantitative and one qualitative items. The levels remain same; Yes, No and Don't Know for the first four items but the fifth item was qualitative, which allows the respondents the freedom to write in brief about what else is/are required to include in their textbooks related to DM.

Study Design

The cross-sectional survey design was used in the present study. Actually, cross-sectional survey gathers information to make derivations about a populace of enthusiasm at one point in time. It has been depicted as previews of the populaces about which they accumulate information. It might be rehashed intermittently; in any case, in a rehashed cross-sectional survey, respondents to the study at one point in time are not purposefully examined once more, in spite of the fact that a respondent to one organization of the study could be haphazardly chosen for a consequent one. Cross-sectional surveys would thus be able to be stood out from board studies, that is why individual respondents are taken for the long run. Board reviews, for the most part, are directed to gauge the change in the populace being considered.

Procedure

For collecting data for the questionnaire was administered with the help of six separate teams altogether simultaneously. For the urban areas, we chose schools from Dhaka, Chittagong, and Sylhet, and for rural areas Tangail, Bhola, and Satkhira. Since this present study is disaster focused, so we chose the most disaster-prone areas. Respondents were given a brief written instruction along with the questionnaire (28 quantitative items and one qualitative or descriptive item). They were assured verbally that the information collected from them would be strictly confidential and would be used only for disaster-related research. Respondents were asked to read the questionnaire and express their feelings accordingly. They expressed their opinion by putting tick (√) mark in the appropriate response boxes, those boxes which were best fit to their opinion. After completing their task, they were thanked for their cooperation.

Data Analysis

As said in methodology, fundamentally three sorts of dimensions have been investigated through percentage tests to explore general DRR information of high school students in Bangladesh. The impacts of gender orientation and residential difference were taken care of in the analysis by a comparative process (male/female; urban/rural). The collected data on textual knowledge on DM were subjected to percentage tests in order to examine whether there were any differences in gender orientation and residential position on disaster-related textual practical knowledge.

Results are presented in the following sections. Final questionnaire results are given in Tables 9.1 to 9.4. The study revealed some significant and critical factors regarding student perceptions of DM. The findings are very important for disaster-prone areas like Bangladesh. The first analysis

Table 9.3 The overall percentage of all sections

S/No.	Item	Percentage of responses		
		Yes	No	Unknown
1.1	Do you know when a disaster will occur?	70	18	12
1.2	Do you think that disaster cannot be prevented?	55	28	17
1.3	Do you think that there is applicability of taking part in disaster management training	85	1	15
2.1	Do you think that to come across a disaster and remain alive depends on your luck?	70	20	8
2.2	Do you think that there is significance of disseminating textual knowledge and experiences?	77	7	16
2.3	Do you think that government is capable enough to cope with disasters?	69	19	13
2.4	Do you think that government and people are confident and capable for reconstruction activities after disaster?	60	23	17
2.5	Do you think it is necessary to discuss resembling disasters?	82	6	13
2.6	Do you think that it is essential listening to people who work or do activities for disaster management?	73	12	16
2.7	Do you think that there is necessity to disseminate your textual knowledge resembling disasters with others?	66	9	26
3.1	Do you think that it is essential to take shelter at shelter house or shelter center?	85	5	10
3.2	Do you know the information about which government office needs to be contacted after the disaster?	14	75	11
3.3	Do you know the disaster-prone areas of Bangladesh?	24	61	15
3.4	Did you get any information from INGOs/NGOs about disasters?	5	95	0
3.5	Do you have consciousness about evacuation procedures during disasters?	17	81	3
3.6	Do you know the community activities during disasters?	38	47	16

(continued)

Table 9.3 (Continued)

S/No.	Item	Percentage of responses		
		Yes	No	Unknown
3.7	Do you know the life after in state of evacuation after the disasters?	29	51	21
4.1	Do you think that volunteer's role in necessary to mitigate disasters?	68	14	19
4.2	Do you think that enforcing building is important to escape from disasters?	91	4	6
4.3	Do you think that preparing emergency bag is important to subsidize disasters?	86	5	10
4.4	Do you think that it is important to be good with community from everyone's side to mitigate the disasters?	80	11	9
4.5	Do you think that repair of road blockage and transportation breaks must be as soon as possible after disasters?	75	10	16
4.6	Do you think that it is important to build disaster awareness in local, regional, and national level?	28	46	26
4.7	Do you think that rapid rehabilitation is necessary after disasters?	69	15	16
5.1	Do you think large-scale disasters will certainly occur in Bangladesh in next 10 years?	43	43	15
5.2	Do you think your area is safe from all kinds of disasters?	39	38	23
5.3	Do you think your building is well designed and will withstand an earthquake event?	26	50	24
5.4	Do you have any idea about security of sleeping space?	12	70	18
6.1	Do you think your knowledge of disaster is textual?	16	68	18
6.2	Do you think your textual knowledge on disaster is applicable to practical scale?	30	48	23
6.3	Do you think your textual knowledge regarding disaster is adequate?	18	54	28
6.4	Do you think your textual disaster-related knowledge is applicable during an emergency?	25	44	31

is on the basis of overall situation of knowledge of disaster and its management, where 30.2 percent of the participants are aware of disasters, 29.9 percent think that they are ready to deal with disasters, 22.1 percent think that the knowledge of preparing disaster in their textbooks and dealing with disasters is adequate. The eventual result for the overall percentages of all sections is presented in Table 9.3.

As we have six particular sections of the questionnaire, we have analyzed each section separately.

Disaster-Related Concerns in which we have conducted study of overall knowledge and concern toward sustainable DM. For this particular section, we have found 96.7 percent as positive response. The next section is Readiness Behavior; where we have found 70.8 percent to be positive, Yes-type response. For the Adaptation with Disasters section; we have found 70.9 percent positive response from the participants. For the Disaster Awareness section; we have found alarmingly just 30.2 percent positive, Yes-type responses. The next one is Disaster Risk Preparations, where we have found 29.9 percent positive response. For the last section, Textual Knowledge, we have found less positive feedback, which is 22.1 percent. The overall result for all sections has been presented in Table 9.4.

Table 9.4 The overall results by sections

		Percentage of responses		
S/No.	Concerns	Yes	No	Unknown
1	Disaster-Related Concerns	69.7	15.7	14.6
2	Readiness Behavior	70.8	13.7	15.5
3	Adaptations with Disasters	70.9	14.7	14.4
4	Disaster Awareness	30.2	59.1	10.7
5	Disaster Risk Preparations	29.9	50.2	19.9
6	Textual Knowledge	22.1	53.2	24.7

In the present study, we have also laid emphasize upon the gender difference in all the sections. We have found for Disaster-Related Concerns 73.2 percent responded Yes for boy; on the other hand, 67.1 percent responded Yes for girl. For the section Readiness Behavior, 74.2 percent responded Yes for boy; on the other hand, 67.1 percent responded Yes for girl. For the Adaptation with Disasters section; 76.4 percent responded Yes for boy; on the other hand, 65.3 percent responded Yes for girl. For the Disaster Awareness section, 34.2 percent responded Yes and 58.2 percent responded No for boy; on the other hand, 26.2 percent Yes and 60.1 percent No for girl. For the Disaster Risk Preparations section, 34 percent responded Yes and 45.5 percent No for boy; on the other hand, 25.7 percent Yes and 54.9 percent No for girl. For the last section, Textual Knowledge, 27 percent responded Yes and 52.3 percent No for boy; on the other hand, 17 percent Yes and 54 percent No for girl.

The results for the gender difference factor of the present study have been presented in Table 9.5.

Table 9.5 Gender differences

S/No.	Concerns	Male (%)			Female (%)		
		Yes	No	Unknown	Yes	No	Unknown
1	Disaster-Related Concerns	73.2	18.7	8.1	67.1	13.5	19.4
2	Readiness Behavior	74.2	13.4	11.6	67.1	13.5	19.4
3	Adaptation with Disasters	76.4	15.2	8.4	65.3	14.3	20.4
4	Disaster Awareness	34.2	58.2	7.6	26.2	60.1	13.7
5	Disaster Risk Preparations	34	45.5	20.5	25.7	54.9	19.4
6	Textual Knowledge	27	52.3	20.8	17	54	29

To cover all the dimensions, we have added the residential factor (urban/rural) where we found significant differences. In the *Disaster-Related Concerns* section, participants from urban areas responded 80.5 percent Yes and those from rural areas responded 58.8 percent Yes; in the *Readiness Behavior* section, from urban 71.7 percent and from rural areas 69.7 percent responded Yes; in the *Adaptations to Disasters* section, 78.2 percent from urban areas and 63.5 percent from rural areas responded Yes; in the *Disaster Awareness* section, 38.4 percent from urban areas and 22 percent from rural areas responded Yes; in the *Disaster Risk Preparations* section, 39.3 percent from urban and 20.5 percent from rural areas responded Yes; and in the Textual Knowledge section, 24.2 percent from urban, and 19.9 percent from rural areas responded Yes. The residential differences are shown in Table 9.6.

Table 9.6 *Residential differences by percentage*

S/N	Concerns	Urban (%)			Rural (%)		
		Yes	No	Unknown	Yes	No	Unknown
1	Disaster-Related Concerns	80.5	10.2	9.3	58.8	21.3	19.9
2	Readiness Behavior	71.7	16.6	11.7	69.7	10.6	19.7
3	Adaptations with Disasters	78.2	10.9	10.9	63.5	18.6	17.9
4	Disaster Awareness	38.4	52.6	9	22	65.7	12.3
5	Disaster Risk Preparations	39.3	41	19.7	20.5	59.5	20
6	Textual Knowledge	24.4	56	19.6	19.9	50.8	30.3

Table 9.7 *Response regarding to the open-ended question (multiple responses)*

Responses	Percentage (%)
Should include......	
protection of resources including agricultural land, forests, communication infrastructure and residence	45.25
information about first aid training	43.5
detail information about shelters and food management training during the disasters	40.5
detail knowledge of evacuation procedure	25.75
information about process of relief distribution	24
history of previous disasters	14.5

From the responses to the open-ended question, the respondents' recommendations are shown in Table 9.7. Besides these, they recommended an extensive training program along with textbook knowledge about DRR. In the open-ended question, they have asked whether they are satisfied with the textbook knowledge along with the sustainable solution. In response, they have informed us that the textbook knowledge is inadequate and that they need practical training and orientation as well.

Discussion

The present study was conducted to uncover the significance of understanding DM and of DRR knowledge among the high school students of both urban and rural zones of Bangladesh. For DM and DRR knowledge, we have focused on the youth of the general populace since they are easier to shape in the building of DM practices alongside sound information of DRR. Children and youth are the part of the population that are most severely affected by disasters, as they can easily panic and become difficult to manage during emergencies or crises, especially when a school or a house catches fire (Hassanain 2006). As per the educational institutions and other developmental agencies (e.g., INGO, NGO, UN), organizations guarantee that the DM and DRR concept is being implemented within the national educational curriculum of Bangladesh. All high school students and some at the primary level are picking up the learning about the importance of these key issues.

The present study was intended to identify any viable knowledge gaps as introduced in the national educational modules of Bangladesh for the high school students regarding DM and DRR information. In other words, is the learning, which is guaranteed by the government and other developmental agencies, appropriate or does it provide practical knowledge that can be applied when required? Sufficiency of DRR knowledge comes into question when the practicality comes to be the concern. So, the present study was conducted to explore the sufficiency of DRR knowledge.

The research findings suggest some noteworthy and alarming results in respect of the overall percentage. For example, 30.2 percent of aggregate examination populace were disaster aware; 29.9 percent were prepared with the challenges of DM and DRR, and 22.1 percent were satisfied with the textual knowledge regarding the DM and DRR knowledge incorporated in their educational programs. Actually the 30.2 percent of study population who are disaster aware are well-informed about disaster and its aftermath but they are not properly ready to take all the challenges to manage the disasters. The main role of this population is to assist the mainstream operation mainly operated by the Ministry of Disaster Management and several other agencies, that is, Fire Service and Civil Defense, Bangladesh Armed Forces. Another alarming part is just 29.9 percent of the population are ready to take any challenges to manage the disasters and assist the responsible departments of Bangladesh. The willingness of the youth of Bangladesh is enormous but the question is how much efficient they are! Since they are acting as the active agents and first party responders, so the government of Bangladesh took that seriously and is providing them with proper training through the urban volunteer's program. Again, it has been highlighted that the resources of the government are limited here, so it is quite difficult to bring each and every student under the training program. So, for generalized information dissemination, textbook knowledge is most effective. Unfortunately, the gradual DM knowledge in the textbooks of Bangladesh is not up to the mark and many things remain unclear to the students. They remain unaware: only 22.1 percent students responded as satisfied with the textbook knowledge regarding DM and climate change matters. If we deeply investigate then it will be revealed that this 22.1 percent have already received training, so they have a clear idea of DM although the textbook knowledge is not clear to their counterparts. Almost each and every high school student expect practical knowledge alongside the textbook knowledge for at least their self-defense during the course of natural and man-made disasters. And there is the strong correlation we have found between the textbook knowledge and disaster preparedness. For the other three sections, Disaster-Related Concerns, Readiness Behavior, Adaptations with Disasters, Disaster Awareness seems to be workable for now for the overall study population. Results suggested some noteworthy and alarming findings, for example in respect of the overall percentage, 30.2 percent of aggregate examination populace were disaster aware; 29.9 percent were prepared with the challenges of DM and DRR, and 22.1 percent were satisfied with the textual knowledge regarding the DM and DRR knowledge incorporated in their educational programs. For the other three sections, Disaster-Related Concerns, Readiness Behavior, Adaptations with Disasters, Disaster Awareness seems to be alright for now for the overall study population.

Females are now in typical circumstances: more vulnerable, more burdened, more avoided from basic leadership, decision–making, and over the courses of any. For any nations amid the disasters, they are vulnerable to sexual assault, prostitution, and even child marriage to diminish the part to encourage. Also, that is the reason the misfortune rate is equivalently more than their male partner. Despite the fact that the world is looking for an indiscriminative domain, however, for the underdeveloped and developing nations like Bangladesh girls are helpless and denied in all means. For the poor socioeconomic conditions, the girls remain neglected so they never are the part of preparedness for disasters, that is, swimming, search and rescue operations, climbing tree. These current sexual orientation disparities are additionally found in the disaster readiness phase. The guardians let not enable their girls to participate in preparing or readiness measures while they are extremely ready for their male one. The readiness ought to be sans predisposition on the grounds that every single one of the general public could contribute over the courses of disasters. But because of these social stigmas, we have found that the girls are backward in disaster preparedness and the frequency or rate is quite significant. In gender differences related analysis for section by section, Disaster-Related Concerns 73.2 percent responded as Yes for boy; on the other hand, 67.1 percent Yes for girl. For Readiness Behavior section 74.2 percent responded as Yes for boy; on the other hand, 67.1 percent responded Yes for the girl. For the Adaptation with Disasters section; 76.4 percent responded as Yes for boy; on the other hand, 65.3 percent responded Yes for girl. For the Disaster Awareness section, 34.2 percent responded Yes and 58.2 percent responded No for boy; on the other hand, 26.2 percent responded Yes and 60.1 percent responded No for girl. For the Disaster Risk Preparations section, 34 percent responded Yes and 45.5 percent responded No for boy; on the other hand, 25.7 percent responded Yes and 54.9 percent responded No for girl. For the last section, Textual Knowledge, 27 percent responded Yes and 52.3 percent responded No for boy; on the other hand, 17 percent responded Yes and 54 percent responded No for girl. From this, it is clearly illustrated that male or boy's knowledge over DM and DRR is better than the female or girl students. In every section, we have seen some notable differences among two groups. The matter DRR and DM is knowledge-based and training–driven, so incorporating with the training program/s essential for the learners to become a significant community volunteer or active member of DM. But we have seen the reluctance of the female or girls to be incorporated with such. Besides, the dependency mentality of the female and protective mentality of male lead to such gender differences in DM and DRR.

Differences in residence type indicate that, for Disaster-Related Concerns had 80.5 percent yes responses for urban study sample; on the other hand, 58.8 percent rural study sample responded yes. In Readiness Behavior section, there were 71.7 percent yes responses for urban study sample; on the other hand, 69.7 percent rural study sample responded yes. For the Adaptation with Disasters section, there were 78.2 percent yes responses for urban study sample; on the other hand, 63.5 percent rural study sample responded yes. For the Disaster Awareness section, 38.4 percent yes, and 52.6 percent no responses for urban study sample; on the other hand, 22 percent yes and 65.7 percent no responses for rural sample. In the Disaster Risk Preparations section, 39.3 percent yes and 41 percent no responses for urban sample; on the other hand, 20.57 percent yes and 59.5 percent no responses for rural sample. For the last section, Textual Knowledge, there were 24.4 percent yes and 56 percent no responses for urban study sample; on the other hand, 19.9 percent yes; 50.8 percent no responses for rural sample. From this result, it is clearly illustrated that urban student's knowledge over DM and DRR is better than the rural area's students. In every section, we have seen some notable differences among two groups. But the three sections Disaster-Related Concerns, Disaster Awareness, and Disaster Risk Preparations are more conflicting with their results because the differences are 21.7 percent; 16.4 percent, and 18.8 percent, respectively. For the last couple of decades, the concepts of disaster resilience and disaster preparedness gained several dimensions. Although it was only the humanitarian concept but now the concept is beyond that. It turns into political, social, and economic dimensions to some extent. Because of this continuous mode-changing procedures, media has taken a vital initiative to make people aware of adopting to disasters. For developing countries like Bangladesh, lack of resources also hinders the easy access to media for the rural areas. Even today most of the rural people from this country have no access to satellite television. Besides, understanding the complexities of urbanization numbers of research have been conducted for the urban areas. Since the urban residence is more complex than that of rural, so the resilience modules also developed there carefully. Again, we have to address the matter of resource lacking because the disaster preparedness and resilience in urban areas depend on the mobilization of financial or economic capital and in contrast for the rural areas it is the social capital which works in real. So, strategically the people from urban areas are more disaster-ready and resilient than that of rural areas and that matter is clearly illustrated in this particular result section.

Yet, there was one thing common for all participants—male or female, urban or rural—and that is of textbook knowledge. This is a concern. The results clearly and significantly showed that irrespective of gender or residential status everybody believes that the textbook knowledge on DM and DRR are inadequate. As stated in many of the comment further training of a more practical manner is wanted. Application as well as knowledge is required.

Conclusion

The present study aimed at uncovering the DM and DRR knowledge among high school students of both urban and rural areas of Bangladesh. It also investigated the discrepancy within textbook knowledge regarding the DM and DRR among the high school students from both urban and rural areas of Bangladesh. Study results show, 30.2 percent of aggregate examination populace were disaster aware; 29.9 percent were prepared with the challenges of DM and DRR, and 22.1 percent were satisfied with the textual knowledge regarding the DM and DRR knowledge incorporated in their educational programs. For the other three sections, Disaster-Related Concerns, Readiness Behavior, Adaptations with Disasters, Disaster Awareness seems to be alright for now for the overall study population. We observed significant differences on the basis of gender and residential location. Although the males and the respondents from urban areas found more front forwarding toward DM but there was one thing common for all of male, female, urban, or rural and that is of textual knowledge. Since this is the main concern for the present study, where only Textual Knowledge clearly and significantly showed that everybody believes irrespective of gender that the textual knowledge on DM and DRR are inadequate for practical situations. This happened mostly because of the man-made disasters. For last couple of the years the students and dwellers of urban areas have experienced enormous man-made disasters than the rural areas. So the preparedness among these areas is better than the rural areas. The positivity toward DM was found more among male students because of their participation in DM and DRR-related voluntary works more than female students. This is not a matter of negligence from female students' side. Whereas the participation of male students is more expected due to the social mechanism. Another important factor was residential difference, where we have found the positivity of urban area's students were more than the rural areas. So, textbooks need to play a vital role to minimize this knowledge discrepancy.

Recommendations

Some recommendations, in light of the responses in the open-ended questions, are as follows:

A) The illustrations in the high school textbooks related to disaster should be detailed and specific for practice;

B) History of previous disasters and learning must be incorporated;

C) The knowledge of process of relief distribution;

D) During the course of disaster; which agencies to be notified and where is the shelters are located;

E) Sound knowledge of evacuation procedures;

F) Preparing mass measures before striking disaster;

G) When all the measures are operational, which final resources to be mobilized;

H) How to disseminate the early warning;

I) How to be skilled personnel incorporated with the preparation;

J) Protection knowledge of bunds, drain, and damps;

K) Protection of agricultural land, forests, communication infrastructure, and residence;

L) Intensive first aid training;

M) Shelter and food storage management knowledge;

N) Knowledge of the responsibilities of all agencies and authorities;

O) Sound knowledge of post-disaster rehabilitation.

Limitations of the Study

Data has been gathered from six specific regions of Bangladesh. We consider information accumulation was constrained, so its generalizability of the investigation is limited. Cross-sectional survey design yet another constraint. The issue, which confronted more often than not amid the finishing of the survey was a constraint of time. The examination was directed in a constrained day and age of 2.5 months. The sample size needs to be more comprehensive so that the results can be applied to the whole nation. The rural respondents were not as willing to participate as were urban respondents. For the qualitative question; the respondents were reluctant to put down their opinion. We have faced immense problems gathering data from several agencies. While adopting the scale, there were some procedural problems.

References

ADPC & ActionAid Bangladesh. 2010. *Culture of Safety in Schools: Mandatory or a Choice*. Working Paper. ADPC & ActionAid Bangladesh.

Chowdhury, P. P. 2017. *Combating Urban Hazard: A Qualitative Study of Disaster Preparedness in Dhaka, Bangladesh*. Lund, Sweden: Lund University.

Chowdhury, T., M. I. Sarwar, and M. Muhibullah. 2013. "Environmental Education at the School Level in Bangladesh: Observations with Reference to the National Curriculum." *Bangladesh Education Journal* 12, no. 1, pp. 27–36.

Disaster Management Bureau. 2010. *National Plan for Disaster Management 2010–2015*. Disaster Management & Relief Division.

Hassanain, M. 2006. "Towards a Design and Operation of Fire Safe School Facilities." *Disaster Prevention and Management* 15, no. 5, pp. 838–46.

Kagawa, F., and D. Selby. 2014. *Disaster Risk Reduction in the School Curriculum, the Present Potential Role of Development Agencies and the Implications for the Hyogo Framework for Action 2005-2015 Successor*. Kobe, Japan: UNISDR.

Ministry of Finance. 2015. *Bangladesh Economic Report*. Dhaka, Bangladesh: Ministry of Finance. http://www.mof.gov.bd

Ministry of Finance (2017). Bangladesh Economic Report. Dhaka, Bangladesh: Ministry of Finance. Retrieved from MoF website: http://www.mof.gov.bd

Douglas Paton, David Johnston, (2001) "Disasters and communities: vulnerability, resilience and preparedness", *Disaster Prevention and*

Management: An International Journal, 10, no. 4, pp. 270-77, https://doi.org/10.1108/EUM0000000005930

Selby, D., and F. Kagawa. 2012. *Disaster Risk Reduction in School Curricula: Case Studies from Thirty Countries.* Geneva/Paris: UNICEF/UNESCO.

Tuladhar, G., R. Yatabe, R. Dahat, and N. P. Bhandary. 2014. "Knowledge of Disaster Risk Reduction among School Students in Nepal." *Geomatics, Natural Hazards and Risk* 5, no. 3, pp. 190–207. doi:10.1080/19475705.213.809556

United Nations International Strategy for Disaster Reduction. 2005. *Hyogo Framework for Action 2005–2015: Building the Resilience of Nations and Communities to Disasters (HFA).* Kobe, Japan: UNISDR.

Worldometers. 2017. *Bangladesh Population.* http://www.worldometers.info/world-population/bangladesh-population

English Version of DRR Questionnaire for School Students

(Tuladhar et al. 2014)

Dear Student,

You are warmly welcome to this disaster adhering research. In this present research questionnaire, you shall be asked some written questions. You task is to find the best suit among the options Yes/No/Don't Know. I expect that you have understood you task.

Thanks again for extending your warm cooperation towards this research work.

Biographic Information:

Class: _____   Age: _____   Gender: Male: ☐   Female: ☐

Socio-Economic Status: Upper Class ☐   Middle Class ☐   Lower Class: ☐

Locality: Urban: ☐   Rural: ☐

Disaster-Related Concerns

1. Do you know when a disaster will occur?

☐ Yes   ☐ No   ☐ Don't Know

2. Do you think that disaster cannot be prevented?

☐ Yes   ☐ No   ☐ Don't Know

3. Do you think that there is applicability of taking part in disaster management training?

☐ Yes   ☐ No   ☐ Don't Know

Readiness Behavior

4. Do you think that to come across a disaster and remain alive depends on your luck?

☐ Yes ☐ No ☐ Don't Know

5. Do you think that there is significance of disseminating textual knowledge and experiences?

☐ Yes ☐ No ☐ Don't Know

6. Do you think that government is capable enough to cope with disasters?

☐ Yes ☐ No ☐ Don't Know

7. Do you think that government and people are confident and capable for reconstruction activities after disaster?

☐ Yes ☐ No ☐ Don't Know

8. Do you think it is necessary to discuss resembling disasters?

☐ Yes ☐ No ☐ Don't Know

9. Do you think that it is essential listening to people who work or do activities for disaster management?

☐ Yes ☐ No ☐ Don't Know

10. Do you think that there is necessity to disseminate your textual knowledge resembling disasters with others?

☐ Yes ☐ No ☐ Don't Know

Adaptations with Disasters

11. Do you think that it is essential to take shelter at shelter house or shelter center?

☐ Yes ☐ No ☐ Don't Know

12. Do you know the information about which government office needs to be contacted after the disaster?

☐ Yes ☐ No ☐ Don't Know

13. Do you know the disaster-prone areas of Bangladesh?

☐ Yes ☐ No ☐ Don't Know

14. Did you get any information from INGO/NGO about disasters?

☐ Yes ☐ No ☐ Don't Know

15. Do you have consciousness about evacuation procedures during disasters?

☐ Yes ☐ No ☐ Don't Know

16. Do you know the community activities during disasters?

☐ Yes ☐ No ☐ Don't Know

17. Do you know the life after in state of evacuation after the disasters?

☐ Yes ☐ No ☐ Don't Know

Disaster Awareness

18. Do you think that volunteer's role in necessary to mitigate disasters?

☐ Yes ☐ No ☐ Don't Know

19. Do you think that enforcing building is important to escape from disasters?

☐ Yes   ☐ No   ☐ Don't Know

20. Do you think that preparing emergency bag is important to subsidize disasters?

☐ Yes   ☐ No   ☐ Don't Know

21. Do you think that it is important to be good with community from everyone's side to mitigate the disasters?

☐ Yes   ☐ No   ☐ Don't Know

22. Do you think that repair of road blockage and transportation break must be as soon as after disasters?

☐ Yes   ☐ No   ☐ Don't Know

23. Do you think that it is important to build disaster awareness in local, regional and national level?

☐ Yes   ☐ No   ☐ Don't Know

24. Do you think that rapid rehabilitation is necessary after disasters?

☐ Yes   ☐ No   ☐ Don't Know

Disaster Risk Preparations

25. Do you think large-scale disasters will certainly occur in Bangladesh in next 10 years?

☐ Yes   ☐ No   ☐ Don't Know

26. Do you think your area is safe from all kinds of disasters?

☐ Yes   ☐ No   ☐ Don't Know

27. Do you think your building is well designed and will withstand an earthquake event?

☐ Yes   ☐ No   ☐ Don't Know

28. Do you have any idea about security of sleeping space?

☐ Yes   ☐ No   ☐ Don't Know

Textual Knowledge

29. Do you think your knowledge of disaster is textual?

☐ Yes   ☐ No   ☐ Don't Know

30. Do you think your textual knowledge on disaster is applicable to practical scale?

☐ Yes   ☐ No   ☐ Don't Know

31. Do you think your textual knowledge regarding disaster is adequate?

☐ Yes   ☐ No   ☐ Don't Know

32. Do you think your textual disaster-related knowledge is applicable during an emergency?

☐ Yes   ☐ No   ☐ Don't Know

33. Which lessons/matters related to disasters are required to include in your textbooks?

☐ Yes   ☐ No   ☐ Don't Know

CHAPTER 10

IT, Sustainable Development Goals, and Disaster Management

Sarfraz Khawaja

(Former Dean) National School of Public Policy,
Lahore, Pakistan

Huong Ha

School of Business, Singapore University of Social Sciences,
Singapore

Ayesha Akbar

National School of Public Policy, Lahore, Pakistan

Introduction

Disaster management by employing technology is a widely acclaimed mechanism to help in building mitigation strategies for preparedness for and responses to disasters. In the same domain, policy design is one of the best vehicles to address the gaps in promoting education and better health care standards, especially in developing countries in South Asia.

Since January 1, 2016, the 17 Sustainable Development Goals (SDGs) by the world leaders in a historic UN summit in September 2015 for the 2030 Agenda for Sustainable Development are universally applicable to all countries to take measures to end poverty, tackle climate change, and fight inequalities (UN 2017).

Pakistan, in order to achieve the agenda of the SDGs, created a national framework to establish a link between modern technology and resource mobilization. The primary initiative is an integration of IT (information technology) to bridge the gaps in service delivery. The breakthrough in technology can be employed with proper integration of policy interventions and used to find loopholes in the administrative system. The transformation of manual records to the digitized "dashboards" (Punjab Information Technology Board [PITB], Government of the Punjab 2017) provides the reflection of the overall performances to target the areas of underperformance or to highlight efficient services. The integrated model of IT offers the capability of designing administrative structures with effective processes to ensure that the SDGs can be attained (Kiani 2017; UN 2017).

The government and relevant stakeholders, with these structural changes, can work out a plan to involve local government actors as they are in close contact with the community. These reforms aim at better communicating the needs of society, and the country at large, to deliver the SDGs. This activity will stimulate more options to improve the indicators of all SDGs, which in turn can help to mitigate disaster risk. Thus, this chapter discusses how Pakistan has tried to achieve the SDGs via the use of IT in many different sectors.

IT and Preparedness Responses to Disaster Management

Public service delivery has witnessed a significant improvement with the integration of IT. It improves the monitoring of service delivery and provides effective means for informed decisions and policy. Pakistan's public sector has not been able to produce acceptable results in the provision of water supply, basic health, primary education, and other public services through good governance. Thus, the government introduced a paradigm shift from traditional to technological models to produce a significant difference in the governance structure, and to ensure that laws are followed. Integration of IT in the service structure of emergency response security staff that includes emergency rescue, fire brigade, and road accidents and such services reflected a significant improvement. IT has developed a nexus in governance and service delivery to assure reliability, predictability, validity, and transparency in the implementation of rules and regulations. These elements strengthen the monitoring and evaluation mechanisms and ensure evidence-based policy creation and decision-making.

Rescue-1122 is a public sector organization run by the state for providing emergency services to deal with the disaster management incidents, and to improve human development (Sriram et al. 2016). This chapter briefly discusses a success story after going through rigorous data collection and deep analysis of the organization. The service delivery model of Rescue-1122 works on two fronts: front-office interface and the back-office interface. Back-office defines the procedures of the operations, and assures the compliance of the staff, whereas front office is equipped with the latest technology and good infrastructure in order to handle the emergency calls. Both ends are integrated with satellite-based vehicle tracking wireless system, fleet monitoring system, and IP camera that monitors every move of the staff for the assurance of efficient services and to identify distortions in the system.

In Pakistan, the standard time of reaching to the emergency location is 7 minutes as provided in the manual of the organization, and drivers "behavior, traffic volumes and the technical assistance being provided to the emergency are monitored by the front-office personnel" (Punjab Emergency Service (Rescue 1122) n.d.). Then, the information is uploaded to the main dashboard of Lahore headquarters from the provincial offices for the 24/7 surveillance. With the adoption of IT, the service cycle has improved the disaster management and emergency case responses significantly thus improving public services.

This innovative model for delivery of public services can be replicated in other public agencies to ensure transparency, identifying the loopholes, developing a redress mechanism, and to generate information for making informed decisions. For example, the management of Rescue-1122 strategized the policies and procedures in such a way to develop a comprehensive model for the integration of technology (Punjab Emergency Service (Rescue 1122 n.d.). This model provides efficient service delivery as well as maintains the standards of the organization.

IT and Education

As education is a catalyst for achieving SDGs, it is important to discuss how IT can help Pakistan discharge its duty via launching several educational initiatives (Ministry of Planning, Development & Reform 2014).

Under *E-learning Initiative*, PITB, in the realization of the need of technology for the management of its administration, introduced a myriad of projects to generate evidence to make decisions. Integration of IT for maneuvering governance strategies has been considered one of the drivers of reforms, and to achieve Goal 4 of the SDGs.

E-learning enables teachers to deliver lectures with the help of sophisticated digital devices (Masic 2008). Android tablets have been handed over to teachers equipped with semi-smart TVs. It helps teachers in developing curriculum, plan training activities, and enables students to have online access to study material by using user-friendly interface. Offline availability of content has also been assured to give students full-access to course content. E-learning aims to make education, including environmental education and disaster education, more accessible by the provision of digitized content, online tools for the evaluation of teachers and students (PITB, Government of the Punjab 2017). It corrects technological gaps, addresses issues of adoption, and upgrades weak content.

Under *Smart Monitoring of Schools*, Punjab Government employs 950 monitoring officers across the province for the monitoring of 52,695 public schools all over Punjab by making spot-visits. This monitoring mechanism is part of the *Open Data Strategy* of Government of Punjab (PITB, Government of the Punjab 2017). During visists teacher presence, student enrolment, and attendance, availability of facilities such as clean drinking water, electricity, and toilets are assured. All the data is placed on the websites of respective schools by summarizing information from the actual monitoring forms to guide the decisions on provincial and district levels.

Literacy and Numeracy Drive is a project of PITB to evaluate the performance of schools (PITB, Government of the Punjab 2017). The program evaluates the performance based on the criteria of pre-designed students learning objectives (SLOs). The designs aim at defining the criteria of structuring school curricula. Monitoring and evaluation assistants have been handed over devices with the installation of applications with a series of tests comprising multiple-choice questions based on SLOs. An average of 49,000 public schools are visited on a monthly basis, with approximately 2,400 visits each day. It means that around 14,000 students are assessed every day (PITB, Government of the Punjab 2017).

Under *IT and Policy Design,* Centre for Economic Research in Pakistan (CERP) (2016) has introduced a mechanism of data-driven insights for policy design in operating the administrative system. The initiative ignites an approach to evidence-based policy making in Pakistan. In an attempt to revitalize Pakistan's overall fabric with the integration of technology, CERP started a project in 2002 with the name of LEAPS (Learning and Educational Achievement in Punjab Schools). The project *focuses on changes in the landscape of Pakistan to synthesis information and inform policy and decisions across the country.* Against all odds of poor statistics of education, CERP (2016) draws the attention of government toward better decision-making and accountability, increasing access to schooling, reform poor performing public schools, reform teacher compensation, and the government acts as an innovator.

Online College Admissions System (OCAS) has been developed to provide students with a secure source of facilitation for admission. It is a convenient, secure, efficient, and reliable access to students for admission in a higher level of education. The solution has been provided by the collaborative relationship of Nine Boards of Intermediate and Secondary Education (BISE), Higher Education Department of Punjab, Bank of Punjab, and PITB (PITB, Government of the Punjab 2017).

The objective of OCAS facilitation is to offer time- and cost-saving strategies with the convenience of submitting an application online. It enhances the time efficiency of an applicant for not paying any physical visit to college with the leverage of applying to a number of colleges from a single spot. A long and tedious system of college applications spanned over a long period of time has been made so conveniently accessible with the successful integration of ICT models (Sarfraz 2011; Sarfraz and Jahanzeb 2017).

Though there is no denying that modern technologies have helped in developing new ways and models to achieve significant successes in the teaching–learning process, but they have added challenges as well. Alvin

Toffler said in 1991: "The illiterate of the twenty first century, will not be those who cannot read and write, but those who cannot learn, unlearn, and relearn" (National Library Board n.d.), and he was correct. A whole generation of those teachers who never touched a computer were forced to unlearn and relearn. Some did and some did not, which is the success rate of inclusion and optimization of IT in education (Khan 2017).

IT and Health Administration

In terms of health care, Pakistan ranks at the bottom for infant and neo-natal mortality. 44 percent children are stunted, and 9.6 million suffer chronic nutrition deprivation (UNICEF 2015). According to UNICEF, compounding the nation's state of poor health, for example, is the toll taken by pneumonia killing approximately 92,000 children annually (UNICEF 2015). Pakistan's ranking in the Maternal Mortality Ratio Index has slipped from 147 in 2014 to 149 in 2015, recording a stagger-ing 276 deaths per 100,000 births (UNICEF 2015).

Technological breakthrough and advancement in health sciences have contributed to a vast improvement of health care systems all over the world. Still, real progress is the achievement of universal health coverage by making medicines and vaccines affordable; and educating women to sexual and reproductive health care and preventing children from dying. After several initiatives, inequalities in health care access still persist (World Health Organization 2007). The health indicators reveal a grim picture, more than six million children still die before their fifth birthday each year, and only half of all women in developing regions have access to the health care they need. Epidemics like HIV/AIDS thrive where fear and discrimination limit people's ability to receive the services they need to live healthy and productive lives (UN 2017).

Under *Reforms towards SDGs Targets,* technologically led solutions to the problems start orientations toward smart monitoring designs and coherent policies for ensuring compliance. The Government of Punjab, in the realization of achieving SDGs, has revitalized the health vision with integrated models of IT to track distortions in the service deliv-ery. The PITB offered IT-centric solutions with the help of the World Bank to consolidate information to maintain the supply chain of drugs, equipment, and the availability of human resources. These initiatives are to be rolled out across Pakistan after receiving successful outcomes (PITB, Government of the Punjab 2017).

Under *Electronic Medical Record and Hospital Information Management System,* electronic record helps in Basic Health Unit (BHU) clustering, ensures health service standards through monitoring and evaluation, maintenance and cleanliness system, health watch, and medicine inventory management system (PDSSP, Government of The Punjab 2008).

District supervisory officers are provided with Android-based smartphones to visit health facilities. They pay a visit to health facilities, and monitor the records of absenteeism, stock-out medicines, and nonfunctional equipment. All the information along with a self-photo of the supervisory officer get uploaded with a map in real time with GPS accuracy of 5 m, and such information is available for use by managers at various levels. All the necessary information is communicated with Health Watch application for effectively solving three key issues of (i) compliance of supervisory officers, (ii) validity of data collected, and (iii) timeliness of data reporting (PDSSP, Government of The Punjab 2008).

Under this e-monitoring initiative, 210 Android (PITB, Government of the Punjab 2017) phones and SIMs with Internet facilities were provided to the district health managers (DHMs). These DHMs follow pre-assigned monthly targets for visiting health care facilities in their respective jurisdictions. The DHMs submit their inspection data through the Health Watch application developed by PITB. The data submitted through the application automatically pops up on a map using GPS in real time. Multiple other reports are available on a web-based dashboard for departmental review and decision-making. The Health Watch program has delivered exceptionally positive results from 2015 to 2017, that is, (i) the dashboard has received more than 110,000[1] entries from the field managers, and (ii) staff attendance has improved from 22 percent to over 90 percent[2] within a year (PITB, Government of the Punjab 2017)

Under *IT and Disease Surveillance System,* health science all over the world is led by administration with IT-centric solutions that are produced

---

[1]https://www.pitb.gov.pk/digital_punjab, (accessed January 23, 2018).
[2]Ibid.

by the Centre for Disease Control and Prevention in the United States. The department uses SatScan (software) and Early Aberration Reporting System (EARS) for preparedness to emergencies and to gather information to facilitate all stakeholders. In 2011, the PITB developed a disease surveillance system in response to the vital outbreak of dengue fever to identify geographical location of waterborne disease of typhoid fever, cholera, leptospirosis, and hepatitis A (PITB, Government of the Punjab 2017).

The need of historical data in an organized manner was highlighted by PITB for the early detection of future outbreaks. The government was unable to take steps for early preparedness and emergency response. To overcome the problems, all the available health outlets of teaching hospitals, headquarters of Rural Health Centers (RHCs) at Tehsil and district levels were equipped with trained staff for data entry and reporting of cases (Callen et al. 2013). Each person was provided with a laptop, internet dongle or any other means of connectivity. These all consolidated information is used to make informed decisions, and to plan interventions to introduce innovative ideas to combat the situation (PITB, Government of the Punjab 2017).

Conclusion

The efficient use of IT can improve the mobilization of resources to achieve sustainable development not only in education but to achieve the rest of the SDGs. Reforms in Pakistan with the adoption of IT will improve the current educational and health situations that can help the country meet the SDGs and to keep up with international development. A public–private partnership, integration of technology and the adoption of the global best pedagogical techniques can give a kick-start to provide a reliable foundation for now and tomorrow.

IT-centric transformation of management systems brought about tremendous benefits for aligning departments in a way to produce maximum output while mobilizing the available resources. Pakistan has revitalized the health system by deploying IT-trained personnel for strengthening the monitoring and evaluation mechanism with smart applications and sophisticated devices. IT-integrated models will ensure transparency and accountability while generating the statistical data to form evidence-based decisions. Fostering innovations for coherent policy design is the global demand that the Government of Pakistan has successfully implemented. However, despite improvements in the governance structure, some problems still persist, which results in noncompliance with the existing system. The government can establish a balanced framework for incorporating the holistic, comprehensive, and coherent system of administration for ensuring human well-being, economic development, and a healthy environment.

References

Callen, M., S. Gulzar, A. Hasanain, A. R. Khan, Y. Khan, and M. Z. Mehmood. September, 2013. "Improving Public Health Delivery in Punjab, Pakistan: Issues and Opportunities." *The Lahore Journal of Economics* 18, pp. 249–69.

Centre for Economic Research in Pakistan (CERP). 2016. *Learning and Educational Achievement in Punjab Schools (LEAPS)*. Lahore, Pakistan: Centre for Economic Research in Pakistan (CERP).

Khan, W. A. 2017. "'IT in Education, Reached? Nowhere!' IT in Education, Reached? Nowhere!" *Pakistan Today*, June 14, 2017.

Kiani, K. 2017. "Sustainable Development: How Far Has Pakistan Come and How Far Do We Have to Go?" *DAWN_SDGs*, April 8, 2017. https://www.dawn.com/news/1360165, (accessed December 12, 2017).

Masic, I. 2008. "E-Learning as New Method of Medical Education." *Acta Informatica Medica* 16, no. 2, pp. 102–17.

Ministry of Planning, Development & Reform. 2014. *Pakistan 2025 One Nation-One Vision Development Programme*. Islamabad, Pakistan: Ministry of Planning, Development & Reform.

National Library Board. (n. d.). *Learn, Unlearn and Relearn*. Singapore: National Library Board.

PDSSP, Government of The Punjab. 2008. *Minimum Service Delivery Standards for Primary and Secondary Health Care in Punjab*. Lahore, Pakistan: PDSSP, Government of The Punjab.

Punjab Emergency Service (Rescue 1122). n.d. *Services Provided by Rescue 1122*. Lahore, Pakistan: Punjab Emergency Service (Rescue 1122).

Punjab Information Technology Board, Government of the Punjab (PITB). 2017. *Health. Punjani: Punjab Information Technology Board, Government of the Punjab*. https://www.pitb.gov.pk/digital_punjab, (accessed June 1, 2018).

Sarfraz, K. 2011. *Good Governance and Result Based Monitoring*. Islamabad, Pakistan: Poorab Academy, pp. 21–24.

Sarfraz, K., and Jahanzeb, W. 2017. "IT Key to Good Governance." In *Governance in South Asia*, eds. R. Basu, and M. S. Rahman, p. 84. Delhi, India: Taylor and Francis.

Sriram, V. M., G. Gururai, J. A. Razzak, R. Naseer, and A. A. Hyder. 2016. "Comparative Analysis of Three Pre-Hospital Emergency Medical Services Organizations in India and Pakistan." *Public Health* 137, pp. 169–75.

UN. 2017. *Sustainable Development Goals*. New York, NY: UN.

UNICEF. 2015. *The State of Children in Pakistan*. Paris, France: UNICEF.

World Health Organization (WHO). 2007. *Health Systems Profile-Pakistan*. Geneva, Switzerland: WHO.

CHAPTER 11

Disaster Risk Management

What Have We Learned from the South Asian Experience?

Sanjeev Kumar Mahajan
Himachal Pradesh University, Shimla, India

Huong Ha
School of Business, Singapore University of Singapore, Singapore

R. Lalitha S. Fernando
Department of Public Administration, University of Sri Jayewardenepura, Nugegoda, Sri Lanka

Introduction

Natural disasters are global incidents that can significantly change South Asia's economic development and people's livelihoods by prolonging and intensifying poverty and resource constraints. There are many causes of natural disasters (US Environmental Protection Agency 2016), and there is no "one-shoe-fits" solution to prevent natural disasters. What we can do is to prepare for disasters and mitigate their negative impacts. The main objective of this volume was to examine issues and challenges associated with disaster risk management in the context of South Asia and discuss how to strengthen the disaster risk management capacities at the regional, national, and international levels. An attempt was made to explore this central theme. The reality nonetheless has emerged contrary to the system in place, in the research studies. Apart from this, the damages resulting out of the natural disasters had strained the development opportunities. In the process, the outcomes of the chapters included in this book reflect the policy initiatives, policy implications in its implementation, and recommendations based on their experiences to tackle issues related to the disaster risk management.

This book consists of nine chapters comprising mostly case studies representing different countries in South Asia. These case studies can be broadly categorized into three themes, namely (i) the process of disaster management at different levels; (ii) psychological and physical impacts of disasters; and (iii) mitigating disaster risk through education and technology, that is, information technology (IT).

This book is an outcome of research carried out by the eminent scholars of South Asian countries in the field of Disaster Risk Management. This book presents the facts of how the different countries manage the disasters. The case studies presented in this book reflect *Reality* vs. *Myth*. In quest to improve the ground-level situations, it is pertinent to understand the interdisciplinary nature of the approaches to tackling the aftermath of disasters. This book provides a framework for making the administration effective—for making the mitigation and rehabilitation program better and securing better life for the citizens.

Lessons Learned—The Way Forward

In spite of all debates, discussions, and statistics presented in different chapters related to disaster risks and events, the focus on people is still not established, leaving them displaced and in utter poverty. Sustainable and inclusive development is a failure in disaster-stricken areas and the affected victims. Hence, a few lessons can be drawn from these chapters. Broadly speaking, first, it can be observed from the outcome of different chapters in this volume that risk disaster management policies, plans, and frameworks of different countries are in place. However, the problem in the South Asian region pertains to the implementation and enforcement of policies and regulations. This is one of the common features in South Asia resulting in persistent challenges to entice coordination and collaboration in disaster risk management among different stakeholders. This is especially true among the marginalized sectors since they might not be able to protect their homes, which increase the risk of their livelihoods of being adversely affected by a hazard (Misomali and McEntire 2008). For example, Chapter 5 by Neena Joseph deals with the perennial problem of sea incursion leading to formidable cleaning challenges and health hazards/threats to the community. Vinay Sharma, Parmod Chandra and Rajat Agrawal authored Chapter 8, dealing with the impact of different disasters on the diversity of medicinal and aromatic plants in a hilly state of India and its consequences on society, economy, livelihood, and ecosystem. Along this line, Chapter 2, contributed by Md. Nurul Momen, maintains that situational awareness is one of the most significant challenges for the protection and safety of people. Therefore, community-based adoption, dependent on communities' priorities, needs, knowledge, and capacities, that seeks to empower people should be on top of the agenda of any debate and discussion regarding disaster risk management. The focus should be on environmental governance, which should be transparent and pro-people.

Second, many authors looked at the impact of disasters on health, especially that of women. Disasters can lead to physical as well as psychological trauma, which has a long-lasting effect on the psycho-physical health of the victims. The experience of going through a natural disaster can bring about psychological disorder, such as past traumatic stress disorder (Mason, Andrews, and Upton 2010). For instance, Chapter 4 by Evelyn Gay, focused on the psychological impact of disasters in India, deals with the factors resulting in psychological distress following a disaster among the survivors and those who assisted them, for example, social workers. This component, especially the mental health of disaster relief workers, seems to be a forgotten aspect of disaster management. Mst. Marzina Begum, in Chapter 6, identified the impact of climate change on women's health in Bangladesh. According to Article 4.f. of the United Nations Framework Convention on Climate Change (UNFCCC 2014), before proposing any new adaptation or mitigation initiatives, every country must assess its impact of health considering together with environmental and economic factors and issues, whereas the United Nations also focuses on the importance of protecting "human health and welfare"

(Khan 2002). Generally, the issue of women and disaster management deserves a more in-depth research as it involves mental health.

Third, the world has recognized that in the present day, disaster risk management cannot take place effectively without employing technology (United Nations 2008). Technology enables countries to formulate mitigation strategies for preparedness responses to disasters in a more effective manner. IT is an efficient way to mobilize the limited resources in a transparent manner at all levels; thus, reducing the gap between and among various groups of stakeholders. In this context, Chapter 9 by Md. Zahir, Akbaruddin Ahmad and Oli Ahmed explore how practical knowledge on climate change and disaster risk management has been included in the high-school textbook and students' perception thereof. In the last chapter by Sarfraz Khawaja, Huong Ha and Ayesha Akbar, it is found that the relevance and significance of IT can lead to better development of risk assessment and developing mitigation strategies. However, with the increase of IT adoption in countries in South Asia and around the world, it has resulted into some challenges too. One of the major challenges is electronic waste (e-waste), which is hazardous and problematic to humankind and the environment as discussed in Chapter 7 (Perkins et al. 2014). This chapter, written by Nahilan Nabila Hoque, is related to how e-waste contains the hazardous substances that can damage public health and the environment. Therefore, good e-waste management practice should be adopted by all countries.

Lastly, clear and well-designed strategies and policies are required to address the challenges of disasters. Such strategies and policies must include "directions (toward sustainability), distribution (inclusiveness), and diversity (multiple approaches, methods, and solutions)" (Herath and Ha 2018, p. 167). Mahfuzal Haque has elaborated the paradigm shift in disaster risk management from traditional relief and rehabilitation to disaster risk reduction in Chapter 3, that is, a new direction in disaster risk management.

Limitations

One of the major limitations of this volume is that not all aspects related to disaster risk management have been dealt by the authors since the scope of disaster risk management is too wide. The second limitation of this volume is that not all countries in the South Asia region have been represented because of many constraints, such as connecting to the experts of the unrepresented countries, lack of time and resources. However, the selected chapters contained in this volume represent and explain a wide range of significant issues associated with disaster risk management. It is expected that the present volume, apart from certain limitations, will encourage the researchers around the globe to carry out further research on the issues dealing with disaster risk management in the South Asian context. Lastly, implementation of policy initiatives needs to be addressed at both the macro and micro levels in future research.

Conclusion

This chapter has identified the main themes presented in the book and lessons learned related to disaster management governance. South Asia is prone to a different range of hazards due to geo-climatic characteristics of the region. Hazards exposure is primarily due to two geographic features of the region: the Himalayan mountain belt and the coastal waters of the Indian Ocean, including Bay of Bengal and the Arabian Sea (The World Bank 2012). One of the major problems faced by the developing countries is to strike a balance between development and destruction of the environment. It is common to understand that no development can take place without paying a price for environmental damages. It is evident from the chapters that unbalanced development is one of the significant causes of the national disasters. A trade-off between development and environmental protection would lead to an imbalance in the name of development. A balance between development and environment is integral to keeping our "Planet Safe" (United Nations 2015). Apart from this, exposure to natural disasters is driven by numbers from socioeconomic dynamics, including: (i) population growth and density in hazard-prone areas, (ii) economic expansion, and (iii) the focus of economic assets in metropolitan cities and fast growing second-tier cities (World Bank 2012). Hence, mismatched development and environmental factors including climate change are the major factors responsible for the disasters.

Finally, sustainable development is the only key left to all the nations and especially developing countries to grow economically and socially while keeping our earth safe from environmental disasters. The ecological balance of the planet is at the edge and we cannot wait for it to topple. We need to listen to what our "Mother Earth" is telling us with anger now after failed in cautioning us in whispers. Let us move toward a change, at least as it is and not worse than today, for our next generations. Accordingly, all future research should focus on disaster risk management, especially focusing on both natural and man-made disaster risk.

References

Herath, G., and H. Ha. 2018. "Climate Change Management: What Have We Learnt from the Asian Experience?" In *Climate Change Management: Special Topics in the Context of Asia,* ed. H. Ha, pp. 157–76. New York, NY: Business Expert Press.

Khan, S. 2002. *Human Development, Health and Education: Dialogues at the Economic and Social Council.* New York, NY: United Nations Economic and Social Council.

Mason, V., H. Andrews, and D. Upton. 2010. "The Psychological Impact of Exposure to Floods." *Psychology, Health & Medicine* 15, no. 1, pp. 61–73.

Misomali, R., and D. McEntire. 2008. "Rising Disasters and Their Reversal: An Identification of Vulnerability and Ways to Reduce It." In *Disaster Management Handbook,* ed. J. Pinkowski, Chapter 2, pp. 20–34. Boca Raton, FL: Public Administration and Public Policy/ 138 (A Comprehensive Publication Program), CRC Press, Taylor & Francis Group.

Perkins, D. N., M. B. Drisse, T. Nxele, and P. D. Sly. 2014. "E-Waste: A Global Hazard." Annals of Global Health 80, no. 4, pp. 286–95.

UNFCCC (United Nations Framework Convention on Climate Change). 2014. *Kyoto Protocol.* http://unfccc.int/kyoto_protocol/ items/2830.php

United Nations. 2008. *Disaster Preparedness for Effective Response: Guidance and Indicator Package for Implementing Priority Five of the Hyogo Framework.* New York, NY: United Nations.

United Nations. 2015. *Resolution Adopted by the General Assembly on 25 September 2015 - Transforming Our World: The 2030 Agenda for Sustainable Development.* New York, NY: United Nations.

U.S. Environmental Protection Agency. 2016. *Climate Change Indicators: Greenhouse Gases.* Washington, D.C.: US Environmental Protection Agency.

World Bank. 2012. *Disaster Risk Management in South Asia: A Regional Overview.* Washington, D.C.: World Bank.

List of Contributors[1]

Md. Nurul Momen is associate professor in the Department of Public Administration at University of Rajshahi (Bangladesh). He completed his master of philosophy (MPhil) from the University of Bergen in Norway and obtained his doctor of philosophy (PhD) from Sant'Anna School of Advanced Studies in Italy. He has published many articles in international journals and chapters in different books, dealing in a range of debates in public policy and law, governance, and public sector reform in South Asia. He has participated in many national and international seminars, workshops, and conferences and has been a member of several professional networks.

Mahfuzul Haque, a former secretary of the Government of Bangladesh, has been teaching for a decade and half in different public and private universities, taking courses on environment and development, sustainable development, natural resource management, climate change, biodiversity conservation, and natural disaster management. During his decade-long stint at the Ministry of Environment, Forests and Climate Change, he led the official Bangladesh delegation at the Conference of Parties of various conventions, including the UNFCCC, the CBD (Convention on Biological Diversity), Montreal Protocol, Ramsar Convention, and so forth. He was elected as the president of the Montreal Protocol Implementation Committee and vice president of the CBD Bureau based in Montreal, Canada. His latest book titled *Environmental Governance, Emerging Challenges for Bangladesh* looked at the crises of environmental governance in Bangladesh. His recent book published by Routledge, UK in 2016 titled *Governance in South Asia* carried his article on "Shipbreaking Industries in Bangladesh." Published both in print and online by Springer in June 2017, *The Global Encyclopaedia of Public Administration, Public Policy, and Governance* carried his article on "Environmental Governance."

---

[1]The contributors' names are arranged according to the order of the chapters.

Palgrave-Macmillan recently published a book, titled *Disaster Risk Reduction: Community Resilience and Responses that* carried his book chapter "Indigenous Knowledge and Practices in Disaster Management: Experience of the Coastal People of Bangladesh." He can be reached at drmahfuzulhaque@yahoo.com.

Gay Hui Ting Evelyn is lecturer in the School of Business at the Singapore University of Social Sciences (SUSS). She completed her PhD in accounting at Nanyang Technological University, where she was a *Nanyang President's Graduate Scholar*, and her undergraduate studies in accountancy and business management at Singapore Management University (SMU). She has previously taught accounting courses at Singapore Management University. At SUSS and SMU, she has taught courses in auditing and financial accounting. Evelyn's research draws upon psychology theories and mainly uses the experimental research method to examine human behavior. Her research interests include using psychology theories to study topics such as the effects of information disclosure by managers on the judgments of investors, and the effects of accounting regulations on the judgments and decisions of auditors and managers.

Neena Joseph retired in 2016 from the Institute of Management in Government (IMG) after 33 years of service. Currently, she is a freelance trainer, researcher, and consultant. Her current areas of interest are gender management, disaster management, and governance. She continues to be professionally associated with NAPSIPAG (Network of Asia Pacific Schools and Institutes of Public Administration and Governance) and JNU (Jawaharlal Nehru University). Locally, her professional activities continue with Rajagiri Research Institute as a consultant to research programmes, with Kerala State Planning Board as an academic supporter to the Working Group report on Gender and Development, with Kerala Institute of Local Administration as a developer of training modules, with the Cultural Academy for Peace as a consultant for gender-related activities, with panchayats for the development of the gender resource centres, and so forth. Presently, she is an advisory board member of the Centre for Constitutional Rights, Research and Advocacy and trustee of Sakhi Women Resource Centre, Trivandrum. She is a guest faculty in IMG, National University of Advanced Legal Studies, Kerala Institute of Local

Administration, many panchayats, many corporates, and various government departments. She has her master's degree in business administration from Cochin University of Science and Technology and a doctorate from Mahatma Gandhi University. She has authored one book *Gender Related Problems of Women, Women's Empowerment and Panchayati Raj* and has many published articles and research papers to her credit.

Mst. Marzina Begum is associate professor in the Department of Public Administration, University of Rajshahi, Bangladesh. From February 2006 to date, she has been offering different courses, academic research, and providing supervision and consultation for academic activities of the students. Currently, she is responsible for teaching the two courses on "Environment, disaster and sustainability studies" and "Human resource Administration" at this department. She has both a bachelor's degree (BSS) and a master's degree in social science (MSS) from the University of Rajshahi (Bangladesh) and obtained her PhD from the University of Pavia (Italy). Her main area of interest covers disaster management, environmental policy and governance, and climate change. She has published many articles in international renowned journals, and many book chapters in various books. She has participated in many international seminars, workshops, and conferences and has engaged in various research projects. She has also been a member of various professional bodies, journal editorial boards, and civil society organizations. She received the Gro Brundtland Award 2016 from the Tang Foundation in Taiwan. She travelled to Norway, Italy, Spain, France, Switzerland, Hungary, Qatar, and India in connection with academic and professional activities.

Nahian Nabila Hoque is barrister of the Honorable Society of Lincoln's Inn, who did her honors and master's degrees in law from University of Northumbria, UK. She is an internationally accredited civil commercial mediator. At present, she is an associate barrister of the Legal Council in Bangladesh. She works closely with policy makers, experts, and concerned agencies of Bangladesh particularly in the field of environmental and labor law, and governance and administration.

Vinay Sharma is an associate professor in the Department of Management Studies, Indian Institute of Technology (IIT) Roorkee, India. He has around 25 years of experience in the areas of business strategy, Blue

Ocean strategy, forest bio-residue management, capability development, market development, brand development, and rural marketing. He is an avid researcher with a number of papers published and conferences attended to his credit. He has also contributed an appendix on rural marketing in the 13th edition of Philip Kotler's *Principles of Marketing* published by Pearson. He can be contacted at vinayfdm@iitr.ac.in.

Pramod Chandra currently works at the Department of Management Studies, IIT Roorkee, India, as a full-time doctoral scholar. His research work focuses on strategic marketing prospects for medicinal and aromatic plants of Uttarakhand through a qualitative research approach. He has around 10 years of working experience in academia and has published several international publications in reputable journals. He can be contacted at pckuniyal@rediffmail.com or pra83.ddm2015@iitr.ac.in.

Rajat Agrawal is an associate professor in the Department of Management Studies, IIT Roorkee, India. He has teaching experience of more than 12 years, besides 2 years of industry experience. He has participated in various national and international conferences and published more than 20 papers in different proceedings and journals. He has contributed chapters in three different books published by IGNOU, Delhi and NIOS, Delhi and has given more than 15 talks on various subjects of rural development and technical and management education. He can be contacted at rajatfdm@iitr.ac.in.

Md. Zahir Ahmed is junior research coordinator of Policy Research Centre bd, Bangladesh. Currently, he is on leave for pursuing his doctoral degree from Northwest Normal University, China. He has completed his bachelor's and master's degrees from the Department of Psychology, University of Dhaka, Bangladesh. Earlier, he has served as assistant researcher of the People's Republic of Bangladesh. His research interests are disaster governance, climate change and adaptation process, gender equality, and environmental governance.

Akbaruddin Ahmad is the Chairman of Policy Research Centre bd, Bangladesh. Besides, he is the chairman (admin) of Network of Asia Pacific Schools and Institutes of Public Administration and Governance (NAPSIPAG). Earlier, he has served several international organizations and universities. He is a renowned author with a number of books and contributes regularly to international publishers and newspapers. His research interests are environmental governance, disaster management, financial management, IT, and governance.

Oli Ahmed is currently working as lecturer, Department of Psychology, University of Chittagong, Bangladesh. He has completed his bachelor's and master's degrees from the Department of Psychology, University of Dhaka, Bangladesh. Earlier, he has served at several government banks of Bangladesh. His research interests are human development, social advancement, and gender equality.

Sarfraz Khawaja has just completed his term as dean, National School of Public Policy (NSPP) Lahore, Pakistan. He has to his credit an illustrious career of serving civil services training institutes, university professor, and researcher at Ministry of Education and UN-related organizations. He received a PhD degree from University of Missouri, USA and then served as a faculty member at the University of Wisconsin, USA. He has been awarded Curator's and Frank S. Louis Fellowship of Missouri University. He also served as a visiting fellow at Harvard University. He has been publishing extensively and is the author of more than a dozen books. He has published several papers on various topics of education, public policy, monitoring, and evaluation. He is a frequent guest speaker at civil service institutes and has been a consultant to the World Bank (WB), Asian Development Bank (ADB), and many international agencies.

Ayesha Akbar has been working as a research associate in a policy think tank Institute of Pakistan. She has done comparative research in the domain of public policy and social issues of national importance. Her areas of interest are civil bureaucracy, public policy, and new public management theories. She has published papers on a series of problems related to the economic backwardness, migration challenges, disaster management, China–Pakistan Economic Corridor (CPEC), and human security. She has also been engaged with the World Health Organization (WHO) on a community development project in planning and monitoring interventions. Effective report writing and data analysis are her proven abilities. She has demonstrated her skills in planning and conducting training programs for senior bureaucrats and technocrats.

About the Authors

Dr. Huong Ha is head, Business Program at School of Business, Singapore University of Social Sciences. She has been affiliated with University of Newcastle, Australia. Her previous positions include dean, director of research and development, deputy course director, chief editor, executive director, business development manager, and the like. She holds a PhD from Monash University (Australia) and a master's degree from National University of Singapore. She was a recipient of a PhD scholarship (Monash University), Temasek scholarship (National University of Singapore), and a scholarship awarded by the United Nations University/International Leadership Academy, and many other scholarships, professional and academic awards, and research-related grants. She has authored or co-edited the following books: (i) Ha, Huong (ed.) (2018). *Climate Change: Special Topics in the Context of Asia*. USA: Business Expert Press; (ii) Ha, Huong (2014). *Change Management for Sustainability*. USA: Business Expert Press; (iii) Ha, Huong (2014). *Land and Disaster Management Strategies in Asia*. H. Ha (Ed.), Springer; (iv) Ha, Huong & Dhakal, T. N. (2013), *Governance Approaches to Mitigation of and Adaptation to Climate Change in Asia*. H. Ha, & T. N. Dhakal (Eds.), Basingstoke: Palgrave Macmillan; and (v) Ha, Huong; Fernando, Lalitha and Mahmood, Amir (2015), *Strategic Disaster Risk Management in Asia*, Springer. She has produced about 80 journal articles, book chapters, conference papers, and articles in encyclopedias. She has been an invited member of (i) the international editorial boards of many international journals/book projects in many countries; (ii) the scientific and/or technical committees of several international conferences in many countries; and (iii) international advisory board of many associations. She has also been a reviewer of many international journals and international conferences.

Professor (Dr.) R. Lalitha S. Fernando serves as a senior professor in the Department of Public Administration and as director of research, Centre of Governance and Public Policy of the University of Sri Jayewardenepura in Sri Lanka, and currently she is the secretary general of the Network of Asia-Pacific Schools and Institutes of Public Administration and Governance. She was awarded the prestigious Commonwealth Academic (internal) Scholarship and awarded the master's in development administration and management by the University of Manchester, United Kingdom. In addition, she was awarded a full-time scholarship to pursue her PhD at Graduate School of Public Administration, National Institute of Development Administration (NIDA), Thailand. She has published a number of papers, book chapters, conference papers, and articles, and has co-edited books related to public management, governance, and environmental management and educational management at both national and international levels.

Sanjeev Kumar Mahajan, PhD, a professor of public administration and dean, Faculty of Social Sciences, Himachal Pradesh University, Shimla (India), has had a brilliant academic career. He was awarded the university medal for standing first in the MA and MPhil programs by the Panjab University, Chandigarh. He has presented research articles at several international/national conferences worldwide. He has authored and co-edited books on public sector, public administration, governance, and financial administration in India. Apart from this, he holds many important administrative positions in the university. His areas of specialization include public enterprises, transport management, financial administration, and disaster-related issues.

Index

OTHER TITLES FROM THE ECONOMICS AND PUBLIC POLICY COLLECTION

Philip Romero, The University of Oregon and
Jeffrey Edwards, North Carolina A&T State University, *Editors*

- *A Primer on Microeconomics, Second Edition, Volume II: Competition and Constraints* by Thomas M. Beveridge
- *A Primer on Microeconomics, Second Edition, Volume I: Fundamentals of Exchange* by Thomas M. Beveridge
- *A Primer on Macroeconomics, Second Edition, Volume II: Policies and Perspectives* by Thomas M. Beveridge
- *A Primer on Macroeconomics, Second Edition, Volume I: Elements and Principles* by Thomas M. Beveridge
- *Macroeconomics, Second Edition, Volume I* by David G. Tuerck
- *Macroeconomics, Second Edition, Volume II* by David G. Tuerck

Announcing the Business Expert Press Digital Library

Concise e-books business students need for classroom and research

This book can also be purchased in an e-book collection by your library as

- *a one-time purchase,*
- *that is owned forever,*
- *allows for simultaneous readers,*
- *has no restrictions on printing, and*
- *can be downloaded as PDFs from within the library community.*

Our digital library collections are a great solution to beat the rising cost of textbooks. E-books can be loaded into their course management systems or onto students' e-book readers.
The **Business Expert Press** digital libraries are very affordable, with no obligation to buy in future years. For more information, please visit **www.businessexpertpress.com/librarians**. To set up a trial in the United States, please email **sales@businessexpertpress.com**.

www.ingramcontent.com/pod-product-compliance
Lightning Source LLC
Chambersburg PA
CBHW061211220326
41599CB00025B/4600